# Complete works
# Gaudí

# Complete works
# Gaudí

To silvia

H.A.K.

H KLICZKOWSKI

＊ Idea and concept: paco asensio, hugo kliczkowski

Authors: aurora cuito, cristina montes

Translation and proofreading: juliet king

Art director: mireia casanovas soley

Graphic design: emma termes parera

Layout: soti mas-bagà

Photographers: roger casas, joana furió, luís gueilburt, pere planells,
        pepe buz, miquel tres and gabriel vicens

Copyright for the international edition:
© H Kliczkowski-Onlybook, S.L.
HK Fundición, 15. Polígono Industrial Santa Ana
28529 Rivas-Vaciamadrid. Madrid
Tel.: +34 916 665 001
Fax: +34 913 012 683
onlybook@onlybook.com
www.onlybook.com

ISBN: 978-84-89439-91-7

Editorial project:

**LOFT** Publications
Via Laietana 32, 4 pis, of.92
08002 Barcelona. Spain
Tel.: +34 932 688 088
Fax: +34 932 687 073
loft@loftpublications.com
www.loftpublications.com

Printed by in China

# Complete works
# Gaudí

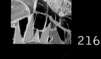

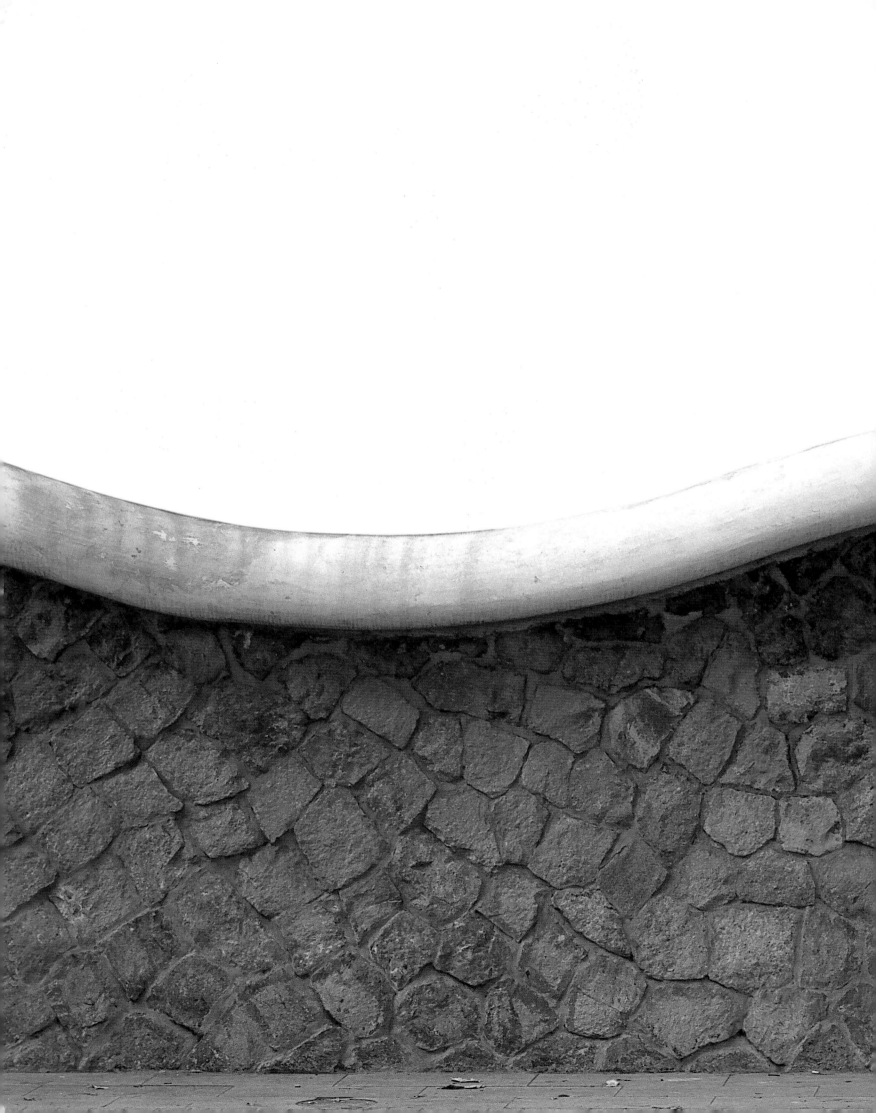

# the gaudí phenomenon

# gaudí: nature, technique and artistry

# The gaudí phenomenon

In light of the growing and general recognition of Gaudí's work, 150 years after his birth, I ponder is the reason for this phenomenon, which is so unusual in the field of architecture. Gaudí did not become a success as a result of the quantity of works completed, since he only directed about 20 important projects. Nor is his success due to the wide geographic diffusion of his buildings, since the majority of them are concentrated in the city of Barcelona. Neither is the architect's fame due to the fact that he was a great promoter of his work and character, since he isolated himself from everything that could disturb his work. Nor were his proposals accepted with enthusiasm by his contemporaries who, in general, were hostile towards them. Therefore, we see that it is not easy to find reasonable answers that justify Gaudí's current notoriety, nor the indifference that he was subjected to, including just before his death in 1926.

Gaudí's secret was probably knowing how to tackle architectural creation in a distinct manner, without artistic or technical prejudices. His knowledge of the trades and the procedures of construction permitted him to stand out in his era. He practiced an eclectic architecture in agreement with the rules of the 19th century and the neo-Romantic and baroque tastes of Modernism. Gaudí was as distinguished a figure as Domènech i Montaner or Puig i Cadafalch, in his most immediate context, or as V. Horta, H. Guimard, C. R. Mackintosh, O. Wagner, J. Hoffman or J. M. Olbrich, at the European level—all architects with grand personalities who formulated their own language and thus occupy important pages in the history of art and architecture. Nevertheless, Gaudí is something more. He is a virile and overwhelming individual, capable of breaking tradition, with fidelity to historic styles and the determination to please the euphoric bourgeoisie of the 1900s. He replanted the essence of architecture and reconsidered tastes and materials, procedures, techniques, systems of calculation, geometric repertoires, etc. It's not that he wanted to start from scratch: by dominating the resources of architecture, whether stylis-

tic or technical, he could embark on a personal adventure, based on a playful intuition that allowed him to create works with independence and originality. No one can confirm that Gaudí was a visionary; even though there are people who dare to state it, basing their argument on a hypothetical esotericism of the system of symbols that he used. Gaudí was one of the most illustrious minds in the transition from the 19th to the 20th century. He perceived that it was necessary to end certain neo-medieval Romanticisms that proliferated in Europe during the era. The world was changing and it was necessary to put other systems of life into place, which architecture had to express.

Gaudí obtained the title of architect in 1878, at Barcelona's demanding Escuela Técnica Superior de Arquitectura. His studies, combined with his domination of the language and the materials of the artistic profession —which he learned by his father's side in Reus and at Barcelona's best workshops— led him to create his first projects by trial and error, with neo-Gothic and Arabic remembrances. His experiences culminated in the Vicens house in Barcelona, where he tackled a type of constructional solution that, today, we can confirm is the seed of an unmistakable vocabulary based on warped surfaces, paraboloids and hyperboloids, helical rhythms and the use of a fiery polychrome. This vocabulary stood apart from any style of the past to obey an architecture without isms, an architecture that, as his disciple Martinell said, we can only call "Gaudíism".

In his maturity, Gaudí was inclined towards an empirical work philosophy. This meant that he relied on experience and accepted those things which saw their best moments during the 18th century. The architect's propensity for everything tested probably also came from the "common sense" of rural people from the Tarragona countryside. They are practical people, dedicated to work and to saving resources and energies. For one reason or another, Gaudí reached a point in his career when he put archi-

tectural procedures to the test. He transformed his workshops into laboratories, he worked with experimental models, and he searched for resistant materials (granite, basalt, porphyry, etc.). He proposed undulating walls and ceilings, he opted for oblique columns and was interested in the path of light and the ventilation of buildings. He calculated the structures of his properties with overhead power cable arches. He also used mirrors, photography and non-Euclidean geometry to design his volumes. His audacity surprised many and was understood by few, but resulted in such impressive designs as the crypt of the Colonia Güell, the Pedrera, Park Güell, and the Temple of the Sagrada Família. These works were easily criticized by the public and by certain members of the press, but their unusual force always astonished. Fransesc Pujols, a popular philosopher of the era and a friend of Gaudí, stated that "in all the works of the great Gaudí, what happened was that no one liked them, nor was there anyone who dared to say it to his face, because he had a style that asserted itself without pleasing." This affirmation seems a little out of place today, since Gaudí's projects not only continue to provoke consternation; they have been transformed into cult objects by majority of the world's citizens.

And here we discover Gaudí's survival. Some of his buildings have been declared Historic-Artistic Monuments and Cultural Belongings of World Heritage by UNESCO. Most of them have been restored and rehabilitated, and in many cases, have gone from private to public property. During his lifetime, Gaudí said that Casa Milà, more widely known as the Pedrera, would end up as a big hotel or a congressional palace. His prediction came true in 1996 when a financial group transformed the building into a cultural center. And the Pedrera is not the only building that has changed uses: the coach house pavilions on the Güell estate are today the headquarters of the Real Cátedra Gaudí, attached to the Universitat Politècnica de Catalunya. Palau Güell (residence of his patron), Park

Güell, the Sagrada Família, and the crypt of the Colonia Güell are all open to the public. On the ground floor of the Casa Calvet, there is a restaurant that conserves the original property. Casa Batlló is a convention center that is partially open to the public and, as mentioned previously, the Pedrera is a cultural center that includes an exhibit hall, an auditorium, a period apartment and —in the attic and on the building's terrace roof— a space called Espai Gaudí. The Palacio Episcopal de Astorga houses a museum and the Casa de los Botines in León contains the headquarters of a financial group and a permanent exhibition hall. Finally, "El Capricho" in Comillas now contains a restaurant.

These Gaudí buildings are open to the public thanks to their exceptional personality. Though each one of the works has metamorphosed, Gaudí remains in force. The best way that we could pay homage to the great architect and artist is to visit his buildings and to know his work. Only in this way can we understand the enormous coherency that exists between his constructional systems, his habitable spaces, and his façades and roofs. Because Gaudí is indivisible; because he is the logic of form and the exaltation of art.

**Daniel Giralt-Miracle**
Art historian and critic
General commissioner
of the International Year of Gaudí

# gaudí: nature, technique, and artistry

Gaudí grew up in Camp de Tarragona, a rocky zone planted with vineyards and olive and carob trees. The countryside was dotted with small villages and rocky massifs. Gaudí´s capacity to observe the landscape during his childhood gave him a special vision of the world. His surroundings, including the animals and the plants, brought together all of the laws of construction and structure that the architect needed to create his buildings.

Gaudí's brilliant mind found information and inspiration in nature. For example, the way he placed arches in the attics of his buildings is similar to the skeletons of vertebrates, and the columns of the Sagrada Família branch out like trees (image 5). His sinuous façades, balconies, and walls depict the swell of the sea or the movement of grasslands in the wind. All of Gaudí´s buildings reinterpret the norms that regulate the creation of the universe, comparing the role of the architect to that of creator. Due to his special vision of his profession, Gaudí lived only to design, ignoring the social, family and cultural life around him.

Modernist architects often reproduced floral motifs, though Gaudí's use of nature in his work (images 11 and 12) reflected a global attitude that exceeded the abstractions used in Modernist decorations. In the contemporary international arena, the English Arts & Crafts movement, led by William Morris, infused the arts with a profound respect for nature.

Gaudí relied on the simplicity and immediacy of nature to solve architectural problems. He distrusted complex mathematical calculations and chose Empirical verifications instead. This method lead him to conduct numerous experiments to calculate the load of a structure or the final form of a decoration. His ideal instrument were models built to scale, and he used them in various design processes. For example, he used models to adjust the plaster forms of the chimneys in Casa Batlló and the sculptures of the Sagrada Família.

When Gaudí needed something more than prototypes to help him advance a project, he invented new models of verification. The most innovative was a model that consisted of a framework of cords with sacks of pellets hanging from them. The weight of the metal was proportional to the weight that the building had to support. Thus, by observing the form of the cords, he could draw the distribution of the columns and arches. Gaudí used this method successfully in the crypt of the

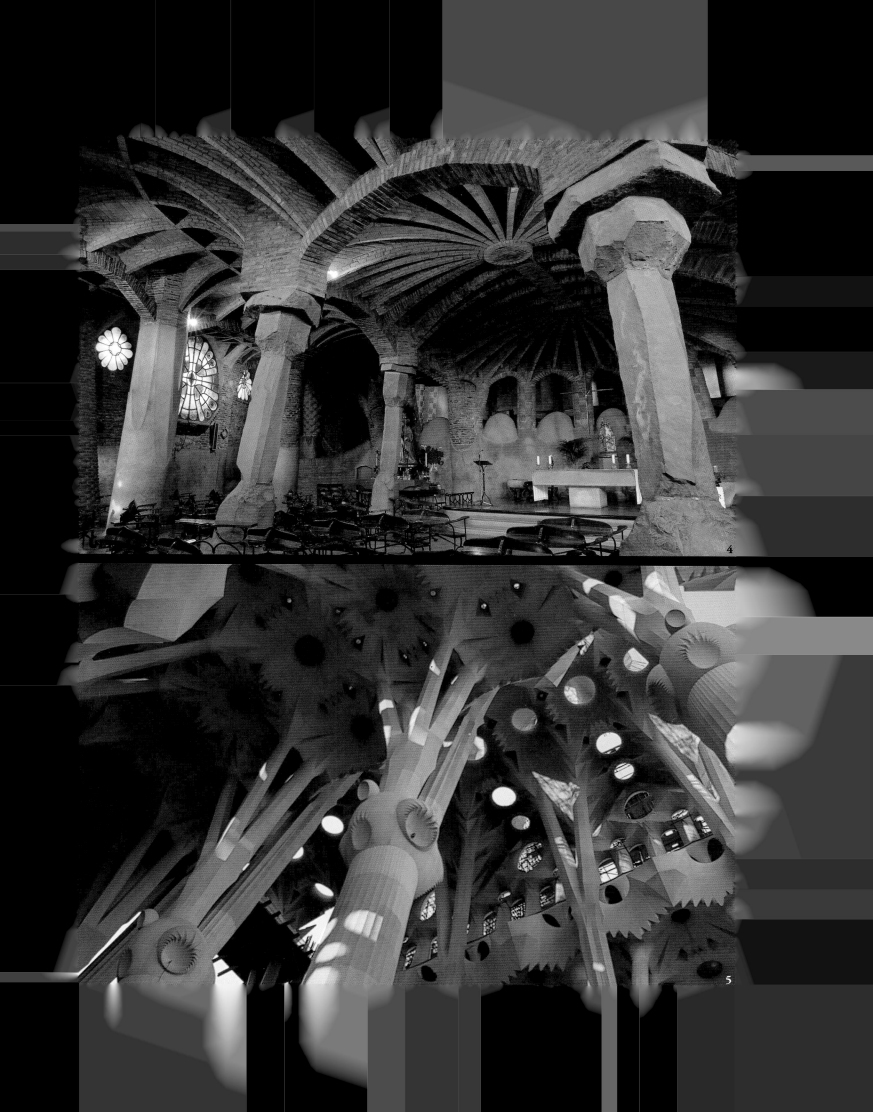

4

5

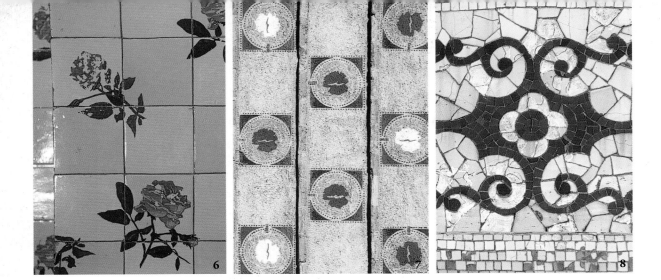

Colonia Güell (image 4), where he built what he had observed in the model to life-size scale.

Gaudí's passion for organic structures explains the absence of reinforced concrete and steel in his buildings. These materials are only valuable when using numerical calculations. Gaudí's brilliant construction ideas could only be realized with materials like wood, stone or wrought iron. Therefore, he surrounded himself with artists and artisans who worked exclusively with these materials.

With ceramics (images 6, 7 and 8), Gaudí relied on the invaluable advice of Manel Vicens i Montaner, a celebrated Barcelona ceramist who commissioned the architect to build his residence. On the interior and exterior of the house, there are numerous ceramic friezes with complex reliefs. The masterly use of fired and painted clay can be appreciated in the mosaics that the architect designed for various projects. Gaudí also played with the color of tiles to solve a lighting problem on the interior patio of the Casa Batlló. By graduating the tile's blue finish, the architect succeeded in spreading light uniformly throughout the space.

Filigrees of wrought iron appear in all of Gaudí's works (image 9). The door of the Güell estate (image 10), manufactured by the workshop Vallet i Piqué, is the most emblematic example. Gaudí also used iron for the balconies, railings and lamps of other projects. He treated the industrial material with sensibility, transforming it into dynamic and exquisite forms.

Gaudí´s use of wood also led him to rely on artisans of the era who could transform his imaginative designs into reality. Of particular interest are the doors and screens of the Casa Batlló (image 3), created by Casa y Bardés, and the level ceilings of the Casa Vicens, full of vegetable motifs (images 1 and 2).

The architect and his qualified collaborators also created magnificent works out of other materials like plaster, stone, brick and glass. The innovative applications, the undulating forms and the new functions for which he used the materials simply would not have been possible without the participation of these skilled artisans. His relationship with renowned sculptors, like Carles Mani, Josep Llimona and Llorenç Matamala, also led to spectacular combinations that mesh technique and art.

9

10

the life of gaudí

Antoni Gaudí in 1888, at age 36 (Photograph: Museu Comarcal Salvador Vilaseca, Reus).

# The life of gaudí

On the afternoon of June 7, 1926, a distracted old man, immersed in his thoughts, was wandering around the center of Barcelona. At the corner of Gran Via and Bailèn street, he was struck by a tram.

The victim carried no documentation in his jacket, making it impossible to identify him. Though he was still breathing, his body was badly hurt and covered with blood. He lay on the ground next to the tracks. Mistaken as a beggar, the dying old man was transported by ambulance to Hospital de la Santa Creu, the place where all the city's vagabonds and poor people are taken. Two days after being admitted to the hospital, the old man died from the fatal blow. In a small and depressing room, he passed away, without any descendents.

The man who had died in his seventies without pain or glory was Antoni Gaudí i Cornet, the architect who had spent more than 12 years working —with all his body and soul— on the construction of the great expiatory temple, the Sagrada Família. In a derogatory manner, the temple was sometimes known as "the cathedral of the poor."

Antoni Gaudí was born 74 years earlier in the city of Reus in Tarragona. Reus has since become the second most important city in Catalonia, in terms of the number of residents, and is one of the most active commercial and industrial centers in southern Europe. Throughout the life of the Reus native, two words were used to describe him: genius and madness.

For many of Gaudí's contemporaries who saw his impossible forms take shape, the Catalan architect was no more than a madman with airs of grandeur. Gaudí's boundless imagination invented fantastic structures that became reality thanks to his profound rationalism and architectural knowledge. During his lifetime, some people —though not many— did appreciate his genius, skill and special vision of construction, design and art. These people enjoyed his work and were conscious of the personal language that he created, a language which opened doors to new architectural currents.

On June 25, 1852, a humble family of tinkers, the Gaudí Cornets, received their fifth and last child: Antoni Plàcid Guillem Gaudí i

Barcelona's Plaça Catalunya at the beginning of the 20th Century. Nearly is the church Sant Felip Neri, which the architect usually attended.

Cornet. Gaudí´s older siblings were Rosa (1844-1879), Maria (1845-1850), Francesc (1848-1850) and Francesc (1851-1876). Antoni´s brothers and sisters died young and he was the only child to outlive his parents. Rosa was the only one who married and produced descendents, a girl named of Rosa Egea Gaudí.

Even though Antoni lived to be an old man, he was sickly as a child, and his weak condition deeply affected his infancy and conditioned his habits throughout his life. For example, he had to follow a strict vegetarian diet and to walk as often as possible.

Starting at the age of five, the youngest member of the Gaudí Cornet family suffered severe pains that obliged him to stay at home for long periods of time. Doctors diagnosed his condition as arthritis of the joints. He was often unable to walk and had to get around on a mule. Unlike the other children his age, the small Antoni had to exercise his imagination in order to overcome the burden of his illness.

Instead of running, jumping or playing like the rest of the children, Gaudí quickly learned to understand and to see his surroundings and the world with another pair of eyes. He was deeply attracted to nature and was capable of entertaining himself for hours by contemplating stones, plants, flowers, insects and other animals that populated the rural house in which he lived. Despite his poverty and pains, he learned to dream. His imagination created his own universe that, over time, would become reality thanks to architecture.

Gaudí's first glimpse of the school world took place at the nursery school of master Francesc Berenguer (whose son, curiously, would become one of his closest collaborators). The nursery school was located at the top of a house in Reus. Even then, at a very young age, the small Antoni demonstrated his incredible visual sharpness. An anecdote from the era proves that he was a great observer: after the teacher's long explanation of birds and why they have wings to fly, Gaudí replied by saying that the chickens he had seen at his

During his high school years, Gaudí's performance was not remarkable; in fact, his student record, which still exists today, shows that the young man failed one or two classes and earned mediocre grades. Withdrawn, solitary, serious, and with a difficult character, Gaudí had a nervous mind. He found it hard to adjust to the authoritarian system, to school discipline and to established norms. During this era, he became strongly attracted to drawing and architecture and had tremendous ability for manual work. He used these skills to make illustrations for the weekly school manuscript and to draw and paint some of the decorations and scenes for the school theater.

With his mind bent on architecture –the activity he would continue for the rest of his lif– Gaudí finished high school and moved to Barcelona to further his studies. At age 21, he was admitted to the Escuela Técnica Superior de Arquitectura. Before being accepted, he had to take a five-year preparatory course for entry. At this time, he was also called for military service. Though it seemed he was destined to join an infantry regiment, he apparently managed to avoid serving in the armed forces.

In 1876, shortly after beginning his architecture studies, his brother Francesc died, followed by his mother a few years later. Dur-

Passeig de Gràcia before Gaudí built Casa Batlló and Casa Milà

house also had wings, but they did not use them to lift in flight, but to run with more speed.

At age 11, Gaudí began his studies at the Escuelas Pías of Reus, a free, religious school located in the old convent of Sant Francesc. Designated for the education of the working classes, the school depended on private donations and on a contract with the local government. It was here that the young Gaudí came to know the Catholic, Apostolic and Roman religions. This is when he probably began to develop his fervent faith, devotion and religion that years later would show up in his Catalan architecture. When Gaudí was already immersed in the construction of the Sagrada Família, a group of ex-alumni from the school of Sant Antoni visited him at the temple. He was said to have assured them that he was proud of having studied at the Escuelas Pías. He said that he discovered there "the value of the divine story of the salvation of man through Christ incarnated and released to the world by the Virgin Mary."

## The way he was

Gaudí's humble origins often influenced his life and behavior. Despite feeling profoundly united to his pueblo and remaining faithful to his origins, Gaudí was attracted to the life of high society during his youth. However, at the end of his days, he lived without luxury and renounced almost everything. He was an authentic dandy who ended up as an ascetic.

Gaudí's features reflected his country roots. He was a well-built man, with pronounced cheekbones, a prominent face and a distinctive nose. His sturdiness was disguised by his blond hair, which was reddish in his youth and then turned white over time. He had rosy skin and deep blue eyes with a penetrating, magnetic and transparent gaze. His impressive Nordic appearance set him apart from his classmates at an early age and stirred rejection in the artist, who rebelled, replying that he was Catalan and Mediterranean.

Though Gaudí had an imposing figure, he was shy and naïve, with a strong and difficult character and temperament. Thought he was conscious of his bad temper, he occasionally unleashed it.

ing the rest of his studies, Gaudí would share living quarters with his father and his niece Rosa Egea, the only family that he had and would have, since he never married.

During those years, economic hardships obliged Gaudí´s father to sell the family property. In order to continue his studies and bring money home, the young architect accepted work with some of the construction masters of Barcelona.

As in high school, Gaudí was not a top student at the university. However, this did not prevent him from obtaining a solid background in architecture and basic knowledge, which he would soon move away from. Academic architecture would serve only as a base for the spectacular and revolutionary concepts that his mind was dreaming up. As a university student, Gaudí received his best grades in the classes of drawing and projects by presenting different proposals than the other students in his class.

In 1878, the director of the Escuela Técnica Superior de Arquitectura sent the student records of four students, including Gaudí, to the rector of the university asking that they receive the title of architect. With his diploma in hand, Gaudí was beginning to be in demand, and he completed a diverse array of assignments after graduation. He designed everything from a kiosk and a wall to a wrought iron gate and a roof with columns for the theater of Sant Gervasi (a pueblo that would later be annexed to the city of Barcelona). Gaudí also designed a glass showcase for the store of the glove manufacturer, Esteve Comella. The piece was exhibited at the Spanish Pavilion of the Universal Exhibition of Paris in 1878.

Plaça Reial in Barcelona, before Antoni Gaudí had designed the streetlamps that still exist today.

Near this location, la Rambla dels Caputxins, Gaudí constructed an urban palace for his patron, the industrialist Eugeni Güell.

The same year Gaudí graduated from university, Barcelona's City Hall selected him to design gas lampposts that were used for street lighting. Gaudí created the streetlamps with six arms that are currently found in Barcelona's Plaça Reial and others with three arms located in Pla de Palau. This would be the only work that Gaudí would do for the Barcelona consortium, since they had a disagreement after the project was finished that closed the door to Gaudí´s participation in future municipal contests.

Gaudí's first big assignment came from Salvador Pagès, a worker born in Reus who amassed a large fortune in the USA. Pagès was director of the worker's cooperative of Mataró and he wanted to build a residential development of individual homes for the workers in the coastal town, located 30 km. from Barcelona. Gaudí proved that he was the best professional to do the job. The young architect designed a perfect urbanistic plan. However, he was only able to build a small part of the project, which deeply disappointed him. Nevertheless, the project was presented at the Universal Exhibition of Paris in 1878, which helped Gaudí become known. From then on, Gaudí was awarded more important assignments from wealthier clients. His workload increased considerably and the hardship that he had known throughout his life ended, at least for the moment.

One of Gaudí's strongpoints was his experience. While studying, he had worked with professor Villar and had collaborated with the architect Josep Fontseré on various projects for the Parc de la Ciutadella. However, the person who had helped him most was Joan Martorell. A veteran architect, Martorell was aware of his assistant and protégé's potential and talent; he opened the doors for Gaudí to a new life. Martorell presented the architect to the man who would become his patron and one of his best friends and clients: Eusebi Güell i Bacigalupi. Güell's confidence in Gaudí meant that other important members of Barcelona's bourgeoisie would eventually entrust him with different projects.

Eusebi Güell was the son Joan Güell Ferrer, one of the driving forces behind Catalan industry and a leader of Catalan economic thought. From his maternal side, he inherited a passion for arts and culture. Eusebi Güell understood music, sculpture and painting; he liked to travel and to discover museums and foreign monuments. So it's not surprising that he went to Paris in 1878 to see the Universal Exhibition and the latest innovations in textile machinery for his business. At the exhibition, a splendid display caught his attention. When he returned to Barcelona, he managed to find out who had designed the works. Shortly thereafter, a friendship blossomed between Güell and Gaudí that lasted until the businessman's death in 1918. No one knew how to understand and to value the architecture of his friend like he did. Though the two men had very different social backgrounds, they shared a similar spirit. They both felt deeply Catalan and their nationalism inspired them to promote the Catalan culture and language whenever they could, including when it was prohibited and persecuted. Whenever possible, they also demanded their rights as Catalans. These nationalist feelings are represented in many of Gaudí's designs, as ornamental and symbolic elements, including sculptures and coats of arms which feature the four bars of the "senyera" (the Catalan flag).

The first assignment that Gaudí accepted from Güell, who become his patron, was a hunting pavilion that Güell wanted to build on some land he owned near Barcelona. Projects of greater magnitude followed, including an urban palace situated near La Rambla in Barcelona, a summer estate, and a colony that the businessman wanted to construct based on the method used for the English worker's colonies built during the era. However, these weren't Gaudí's only assignments, since he never worked for Güell exclusively. The architect alternated buildings for his mentor with other commissions, such as a house for the brick manufacturer Manuel Vicens, a summer residence in Comillas for Máximo Díaz de Quijano, a Theresian school and the Episcopal Palace of Astorga. He also designed a building for Maria Sagués on the land that centuries before was the site of the summer residence of the King Martí I l'Humà, the last Catalan-Aragonese monarch.

## gaudí, a freemason?

Many things have been said about the Catalan architect; however, most of them are nothing more than simple suppositions. Gaudí was called a drug addict, an alchemist, a Templar, and a homosexual.... but there is no evidence that proves any of these labels.

One of the most widespread theories is that he belonged to the Freemasonry. There have been many people who have examined his work looking for details to prove it. Some point to the obsession that Gaudí had for certain elements and others call attention to the fact that he surrounded himself with people who belonged to the masonry lodge, like Eduard i Josep Fontserè, or who were recognized Freemasons. True or not, it's hard to believe that an architect educated at a Christian, Catholic and Apostolic school and who always devoted himself to the design of buildings and religious objects would be capable of living the double life that some believe he had.

The Gran Teatre del Liceu, symbol of the thriving Barcelona bourgeoisie of the era.

Once Gaudí had become a close friend of Güell, he increased his assignments and fees and widened his circle of acquaintances. He entered a prolific period of creative production that eventually led him —with more architectural experience— to create his own personal language. In 1883, his friend Joan Martorell faced a delicate issue: he was looking for a new architect to take over the construction of the temple of the Sagrada Família.

Father Manyanet, the founder of the institute Fills de la Sagrada Família, had already envisioned the temple's design and the first

One thing that is certain about Gaudí is that he was a devoutly religious man who had exceptionally strong feelings of religiousness. Many people have seen in him the figure of an exemplary Christian and a saint. Some time ago, the process for his beatification was set in motion, followed by his sanctification. The Vatican has examined the proposal and has authorized the beatification process. What follows is a long and difficult road to analyze the pros and cons until the Vatican reaches its final conclusion. Whether he will be declared a saint or not, one certainty is that Gaudí's tomb has become a destination for devotees who have converted it into a place of pilgrimage.

tram, he lay on the ground, badly wounded. No one paid attention to the supposed beggar except one man, the textile merchant Ángel Tomás Mohino, whose identity was recently discovered. He and another passerby helped the victim. Tomás Mohino tried to convince some of the taxi drivers who passed by to take the wounded man to a medical center; he had no luck.

Finally taken to a hospital for the poor, the genius died in a desolate room three days after the fatal accident.

stone had been put in place in 1882. Josep Bocabella was in charge of gathering the money for the construction. Since it was an expiatory temple, it could only be financed with money from donations. The architect who was in charge of the project was Francisco de Paula del Villar, Gaudí's former university professor. As soon as the construction of the crypt began, Villar and Bocabella had disagreements and Villar eventually resigned. Joan Martorell —Bocabella's architect assessor at the time— suggested that Gaudí take over the direction of the temple's construction. Bocabella did not object to the solution for two reasons: he fully trusted the veteran architect and, in principle, it was a routine assignment since the plans for the project were totally finished.

Gaudí combined other assignments with the works of the Sagrada Família until 1914, when he dedicated himself exclusively to the construction of the temple. From this date until his death, Gaudí did not accept any other assignments and isolated himself from everything that might distract him from his obsession. He devoted his life to the construction of what, on one occasion, he said would be the "first cathedral of a new series." He even moved his residence right next to the cathedral so that he would save time by not having to commute. The brilliant artist spent his last days immersed in the temple's construction.

Alone, sad, spiritless, and slovenly, the aging architect had dedicated his life to God and to a project with no end in sight. However, his dream was cut short on the 7th of June, 1926 due to an unfortunate accident. As an older man, Gaudí paid so little attention to his appearance that he looked like a tramp. After being hit by a

Antoni Gaudí, in 1924, during the procession of Corpus Christi at the Catedral de Barcelona (Photographs: Brangulí. Arxiu Nacional de Catalunya).

## The International year of gaudí

In commemoration of the 150th anniversary of Antoni Gaudí's birth, Barcelona's City Hall has declared 2002 the International Year of Gaudí. This initiative features many activities which can be enjoyed throughout the year, presenting the special opportunity to know, rediscover or study in depth the work of the Catalan architect. Numerous exhibits, visits to his most emblematic buildings, book editions, CD-ROMs, guides, essays.... even a bus that awaits those who want to enjoy the genius of one of the most important figures in the history of architecture.

constructed works

© Roger Casas

# casa vicens

Carolines, 24-26, Barcelona
1883-1888

*"When I went to take measurements of the site, it was*
*totally covered by small, yellow flowers, which I adopted as*
*an ornamental theme for the ceramics"*

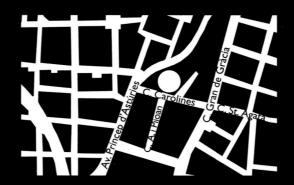

In 1883, a young Gaudí took on one of his first assignments as an architect. Even though Casa Vicens was the work of a beginner, it provided a glimpse of the imagination, sensitivity and skill of the Catalan creator. One can still appreciate in Casa Vicens the rectilinear lines that Gaudí later abandoned in favor of curves and impossible forms. However, the Gaudí touch is definitely present in this ostentatious and unique construction.

Situated at number 24-26 on Carolinas Street in the neighborhood of Gràcia, Casa Vicens is a magnificent building that mixes Spanish architectural forms (inspired by medieval architecture) with elements reminiscent of Arabic culture. The architectural style is more similar to Moorish Art than to the French school, which tended to set the trends of the era.

The tile and brick producer Manuel Vicens commissioned Gaudí to build a summer residence with a garden. The construction site was modest and the house would be surrounded by traditional buildings. These conditions might have caused problems, but they did not stop young Gaudí from giving the project his personal touch and creating a house perfectly suited to its environment. The architect envisioned Casa Vicens as a subtle combination of geometric volumes. Resolved with skill and mastery, the building features horizontal bands on the lower part and vertical lines, accentuated by varnished ceramics as ornamentation, on the upper part.

*The dynamic composition features attractive geometric combinations determined with skill and alternating, repeating chromatic designs*

With a square floor plan and two floors, the building is smaller than it seems. For the exterior walls, Gaudí opted to use simple materials, like ochre-colored natural stone as a base element combined with bricks. The result of this combination is that the brick stands out as a decorative element, as do the multicolored tiles that extend along the wall in a pattern similar to that of a chessboard. The colored ceramics and the small towers give the composition an Arabic feel, which contrasts pleasantly with the window frames, the small balconies and the Modernist forms of the wrought iron garden gates.

When the street was later widened, various elements had to be eliminated, including the arbores, the fountain and part of the garden. In 1925, the architect J.B. Serra de Martínez enlarged the house, respecting as much as possible the criteria, the forms and the colors used by Gaudí. In 1927, Barcelona's City Hall awarded Serra de Martínez the prize for the best building.

Gaudí emulated the Moorish style and resolved one of his first works with great skill. Outstanding features include the striking and generous ceramic ornamentation of the façade and the stunning wrought iron work of the entrance door gate, balconies, banisters and window frames.

© Roger Casas

Lavishly decorated, level ceilings are one of the architect's trademarks. For this room, situated in a gallery connected to the dining room, Gaudí combined two vaults painted with the trompe l´oeil technique. The drawings represent branches of palm trees and two adjacent vaults are also decorated copiously with vegetable motifs.

*With the Vicens House, Gaudí's first residential project in Barcelona, the architect proposed an interesting fusion between architecture and plastic arts. He would repeat this combination throughout his productive and creative career*

The rich decoration used to cover the ceilings and walls demonstrates once again that Gaudí's creative talent had no limit. Diverse forms inspired by vegetable and floral motifs accentuate the decoration of the baroque interiors. For example, in the smoking room, Gaudí covered the walls with papier-mâché, and the level, vaulted ceiling copies the style of Islamic constructions. Each cavity of the vault is covered with plaster and carved to simulate the leaf of a palm tree.

As a constructional solution and in honor of Manuel Vicens i Montaner, the tile manufacturer who entrusted him with the project, Gaudí used glazed ceramics to decorate the walls of the façade as well as many of the residence's interior walls.

Gaudí used varnished ceramics to cover the lower part of the chimney in the dining room and stucco to decorate its hood. For the area between the doors that separate this space from the adjoining gallery, he created large drawings of animals that complement  small, framed decorative fabrics.

# villa quijano-el capricho

Comillas, Santander
1883-1885

*"The owner was called Díaz de Quijano and I said to myself: Quijano, Quijada ... Quijote, better not go there, because we might not understand each other"*

The owner of this property, Máximo Díaz de Quijano, wanted a country house adapted to his needs as a bachelor. This whim caused Villa Quijano to be known as "El Capricho" or "The Caprice." Quijano commissioned Gaudí to make his wish a reality and offered no concept or sketch of the house before its completion.

The construction, located on the outskirts of Comillas (Santander), was isolated in the middle of the countryside among an exuberant and green natural setting. Villa Quijano shares certain characteristics with other projects completed by the architect during this period, including Casa Vicens in Barcelona. However, "El Capricho" demonstrates, at least at first glance, a more restrained and austere manner. There is a definite predominance of curved lines, which begin to steal the show from straight lines. Also present is the architect's desire to combine typical Spanish medieval architecture with oriental elements.

The final result of this medley of styles used by Gaudí is a provocative and personal building. The architect entrusted the villa's construction to his friend Cristòfal Cascante i Colom. Even though an inspired originality runs throughout the interior and exterior, the Catalan architect did not renounce functionality. This is demonstrated by the fact that he paid special attention to the interior spatial organization so that it befits the life and necessities of a bachelor. On the exterior, he also used an inclined roof that adapts to the climactic conditions of the region, where rain is frequent.

The compact building rises up from a solid stone base. The alternating ochre and red-colored bricks are enhanced by rows of green, varnished tiles interspersed with ceramic pieces with reliefs representing sunflowers. The

*The building's natural surroundings define its architectural profile. Tones borrowed from nature create harmonic chromatic contrasts*

strength of the composition is broken by the light and svelte tower that presides over it, but seems to have no apparent function. The tower is elevated above a small lookout formed by the four thick columns that support it. The slim tower is crowned by a unique and diminutive roof sustained by light metal supports that seem to defy the laws of gravity and that give the building the appearance of the typical minarets of Muslim mosques.

Photographs of El Capricho: Pere Planells

A svelte tower rises up from four original columns. The tower has no apparent function, yet dominates the composition. A cylindrical trunk covered with ceramics supports a small wrought iron balustrade crowned by a small shrine.

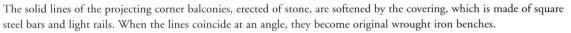

The solid lines of the projecting corner balconies, erected of stone, are softened by the covering, which is made of square steel bars and light rails. When the lines coincide at an angle, they become original wrought iron benches.

The building features some of the characteristic elements of Gaudí's architecture, such as stained glass windows. Two of the windows remain; in one, a bird touch-es a keyboard, and in the other, a dragonfly plucks a guitar. Both are examples of Gaudí's original idea to combine music and architecture in the residence.

Gaudí paid special attention to the interiors of the residence, especially to their organization and decorative details. The spatial distribution is perfectly adapted to the needs of the owner, a young bachelor. The building was purchased by a Japanese group in 1992 that runs a restaurant in the interior called "El Capricho de Gaudí."

Villa Quijano was conceived as a living organism, and the path of the sun determines the daily activities of the residence. The spaces are oriented towards the south, west or north, depending on the activity that takes place and the season of the year.

*Large windows inundate the space with light. Another solution that visually enlarges the rooms are the high, coffered wood ceilings that are true works of art*

# ғinca güell

### Avenida Pedralbes and Avenida Joan XXIII, Barcelona
#### 1884-1887

*"The Door of the Dragon", a masterly work of wrought iron, was inspired by Greek mythology. The dragon is both a decorative figure and the guardian who watches over the Gaudían universe hidden behind the gate*

Eusebi Güell, one of Gaudí's best friends and the principal patron of his work, commissioned the architect in 1884 to construct his estate situated between Les Corts and Sarrià, Barcelona neighborhoods that were then villages on the outskirts. The work entailed rehabilitating some existing buildings and constructing other modules and additional elements, including a enclosing wall with three gates, caretaker's quarters, stables, a fountain, a mirador, the resident chapel and varions decorative objects.

The vast plot of land on which the estate was constructed incorporated three estates, Can Feliu and Baldiró Tower, acquired by Güell in 1870, and Can Cuyàs, purchased in 1883. The architect situated the main entrance of the palatial residence at the Cuyàs estate.

At Güell's request, Gaudí gave great importance to this entrance, which includes two doors —one for people and another for carriages— and is flanked by two pavilions. The volume situated to the left was the caretaker's dwelling. The right side was designated for the stables and was linked to another space used as a manège ring.

The caretaker's quarters were designed as a pavilion distributed in three volumes. The main one has an octagonal floor plan and the two adjacent ones have a rectangular arrangement. The stables

*Gaudí used new architectural languages and discovered vaulted forms that, over time, became common features of his work*

were conceived as a unitary space with a rectangular layout covered with parabolic arches and covered vaults. Thanks to the use of trapezoidal openings, this area enjoys a generous amount of light, which is accentuated by the white color of the walls. Next to this nave is a small room with a quadrangular design and domed roof that is used as an exercise ring.

Between the caretaker's quarters and the stables is a large, wrought iron door that contains the sculpture of a dragon. The workshop Vallet i Piqué handcrafted the piece in 1885 from an imaginative design by Gaudí.

When it came to envisioning the entrance door for carriages, everything indicates that Gaudí found inspiration in Greek mythology, concretely in the legend of the "Garden of the Hesperides." This legend tells the story of three nymphs who were assigned custody of the apples of gold. When they lost them, they were punished and transformed into a tree. The garden in which they were found is watched over by an inhospitable dragon.

Photographs of Finca Güell: Pere Planells

The dome that tops the building of the stables is perforated by numerous openings in the form of windows that achieve a homogeneous illumination in the interior. The dome's covering —colorful ceramic pieces— as well as the finishing touch —a small tower of Arabic inspiration— create a certain baroque feeling that contrasts with the striking red brick and stone forms of the construction.

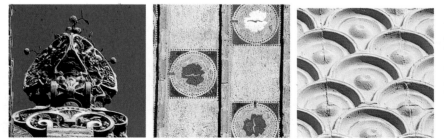

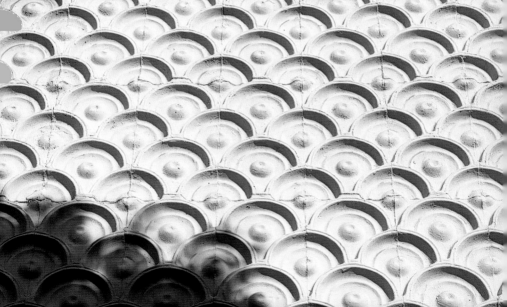

Gaudí unleashed his imagination and genius for the architectural and decorative resources used on the exterior and in the interior. Though the buildings have completely different styles, they are unified, in part, by the ornamental solution used to cover the façades of the stables and the caretaker's flat. Both are adorned with decorative motifs. The semi-circular, abstract elements that cover the exterior walls of these buildings contrast with the sobriety of the brick. They also give the composition a unique oriental style that is reminiscent of the traditional Arabic ornamentation used in Muslim constructions.

The old pavilion of the stables contains the installations of the Real Catédra Gaudí. The space features a rectangular floor plan covered with walled–up vaults and parabolic arches that are linked to another space, the old exercise ring, which has a square floor plan. The floor is made of brick and a wrought iron door that presides over the space is situated under a cross section, also of brick. The light tone of the walls, the flamboyant dome that crowns the roof, and the diverse openings in the walls illuminate the nave in a homogeneous and magnificent way.

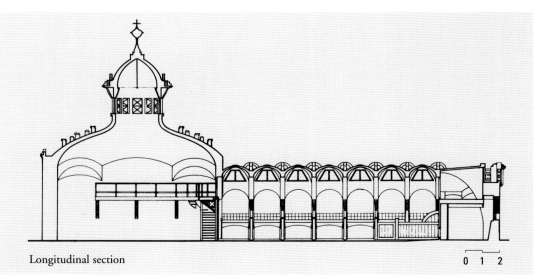

Longitudinal section

0　1　2

Transversal section

0 5 10

© Miquel Tres

# temple of the sagrada família

Plaza de la Sagrada Família, Barcelona

1883-1926

*"The Temple of the Sagrada Família will not be the last cathedral that he constructs, but perhaps it will be the first of a new series"*

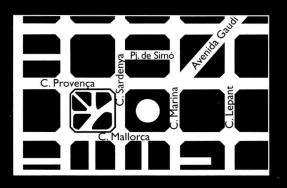

In 1887, the congregation of devotees of San José, led by the bookseller José Maria Bocabella, began the project of constructing a large temple financed with donations. The architect Francisco de Paula del Villar offered to draw up the plans for free. He designed a neo-Gothic church: three naves with a crypt oriented according to the site's orthogonal axis.

The first stone was put into place on March 19, 1882, the festival of San José. Villar abandoned the directorship of the work one year later, after discrepancies with the committee over economic terms, since the project had already exceeded the provisions of the budget. Joan Martorell Montells, director of the committee, recommended that Gaudí, only 31 at the time, take charge of the construction. In 1884, Gaudí signed his first plans: the elevation and the section of the altar of the Chapel of San José, which was inaugurated one year later.

Unlike Villar's neo-Gothic project, Gaudí imagined a church with numerous technical inventions and with a floor plan of the Latin cross placed on top of the initial crypt. Above it, the main altar was surrounded by seven domes dedicated to the pains and sins of San José. The doors of the crossing are dedicated to Passion and the Birth, and the principal façade, which opens onto the street Mallorca, to Glory. Above each façade, Gaudí designed four towers, twelve in total which represent the Apostles. Around the middle one dedicated to Jesus Christ, there are four more dedicated to the evangelists and one to the Virgin. In the numerous portals, Gaudí hung an infinite number of sculptures representing distinct religious figures. The Sagrada Família considers itself to be a stone Bible that reproduces scenes of the life of Jesus and symbols of the Old Testament so that devotees can learn the Catholic creed.

On June 12, 1926, Gaudí was run over by a tram. He died three days later in the at Hospital de la Santa Creu. Since then, champions and critics of the temple have debated its completion. Yet, the construction continues its course thanks to donations from around the world.

*Construction on the church has continued for more than 100 years and the end is still far off*

© Pere Planells

© Pere Planells

The lines of the internal part of the Façade of the Birth, to the right, are much more restrained than the lines of the exterior. The forms are austere, like those of Bodegas Güell; however, in this case, they will be eventually be accompanied by sculptures. The Sagrada Família began with stone from the quarry of Montjuïc, but after its abandonment in 1956, the work continued with artificial stone and concrete.

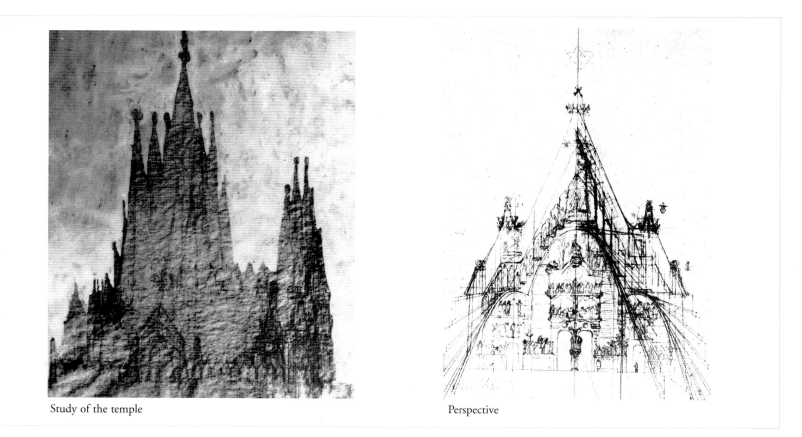

Study of the temple

Perspective

Section

0 3 6

Evolution of the sections

0 2 4

© Pere Planells

The sculptures that the artist designed for the façades of the temple are based on life-sized plaster, mock-ups that Gaudí modeled on people and live animals. A curious example is a Roman soldier from the slaughter of the Innocent Saints that he based on the waiter of a nearby tavern.

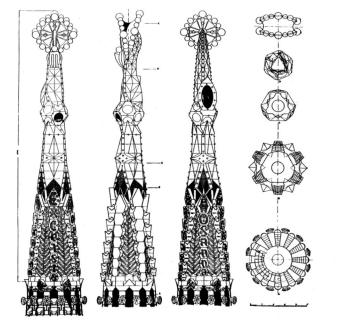

Elevations and sections of the towers

Since it is difficult to replace the pieces that cover the spires of the towers, Gaudí commissioned workers of Murano, in Venice, to create vitreous pieces of mosaic, which are much more resistant. This is one example of the innumerable collaborations of artisans. Gaudí also enlisted the skills of numerous sculptors, including Joan Matamala i Flotats, Llorenç Matamala i Piñol and Jaume Busquets.

# palau güell

Nou de la Rambla, 3-5, Barcelona
1886-1888

*Gaudí found inspiration for the unique dome, which is designed like a
starry sky inside the palace, at the Dome of Saint Sophia in Istanbul.
The dome dominates the space and bathes the large central room in light*

eclared a World Heritage building by UNESCO, Palau Güell —another assignment that Eusebi Güell awarded to his protégé— is the building that permitted Gaudí to abandon anonymity. The architect designed this residence without fear and without budgetary constraints. For its construction, he used the best stones, the best wrought iron work and the best cabinetry, making this house the most expensive building of its time.

The peculiar location of this urban palace, on a tight and narrow street in Barcelona's old quarter, makes it impossible to view the construction as a whole from the exterior. Yet, despite the difficult conditions of the site and the inappropriateness of the zone, Güell decided to construct his residence on this street in order to put his family properties to use.

The sober and austere stone façade does little to warn the visitor of the majestic and opulent interior. This project presents a Gaudí who devoted more attention to the ornamentation of the exterior than in previous projects and who poured imagination into the decoration of the interior, which displays an unprecedented luxury. Gaudí also gave more importance to constructional solutions.

More than 25 designs preceded the definitive façade, which features historical lines and subtle, classic airs reminiscent of traditional Venetian palaces. Two large doors in the form of parabolic arches perforate the façade and provide access for both carriages and pedestrians. The palace includes a basement, four floors and a terrace roof. To reach the cellars, where there is a stable for horses and a room for grooming and equipment, Gaudí created two ramps. The one for service has a helical form and the one for horses has a softer configuration.

The first floor is located at street level and the principal staircase that presides over the entrance is located between two halls. From this landing another staircase leads to the noble floor on which there is an anteroom, a visiting room, a boudoir and a corridor which leads to the hall in which Güell celebrated meetings, concerts, and parties. The terrace roof is reached across a service stairway and is dotted with decorated chimneys that serve as ventilation and smoke exits. For many years, the palace was a social political, and cultural center. During the Civil War (1936-39), anarchists confiscated the residence and used it as a house for troops, with a prison center in the cellars. In 1945, the Diputación acquired it and restored it for the first time.

*Gaudí created a building that aroused astonishment and even rejection for its new constructional solutions*

Photographs of Palau Güell: Pere Planells

Gaudí had little respect for proportion and constantly played with optical illusions and architectural solutions that tricked the visitor into believing that a space was larger than it actually was. An example of this is the impressive 56-foot hight central hall, a space elevated with mastery from the ground floor all the way up to the building's top floor.

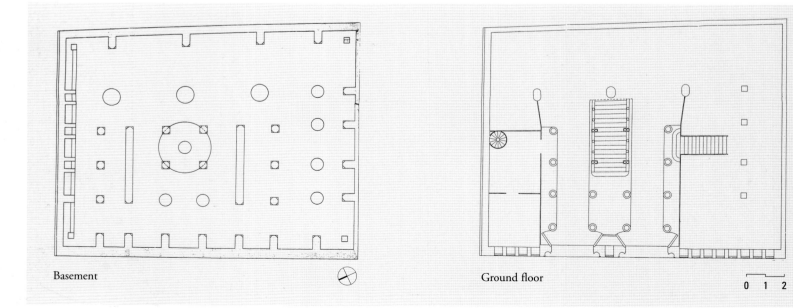

Basement

Ground floor

0  1  2

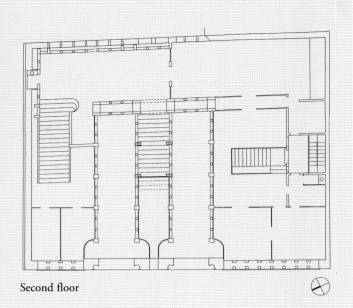

Second floor

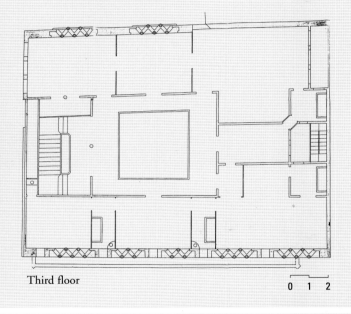

Third floor

0  1  2

The terrace roof is a distinctive element of Güell Palace and would later have an even more important role in the Pedrera. Using his imagination, Gaudí drew an imaginative rooftop with impossible forms. The volumes have a decorative and sculptural power, as well as a practical function, since they serve are chimneys and ventilation ducts for the building. In order to dress up these functional elements, Gaudí used brick for the chimneys and ventilation ducts connected to the spaces used for the service and for the kitchens. To cover those coming from the areas used by the Güell family and their guests, Gaudí used "trencadís" (pieces of multi-colored tile).

# palacio episcopal de Astorga

Plaza Eduardo de Castro, 24, Astorga, León
1889-1893

*"In modern architecture, the Gothic style must be a starting point but never the ending point."*

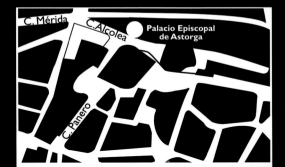

After a devastating fire completely destroyed the Episcopal Palace of Astorga, the bishop Juan Bautista Grau i Vallespinós commissioned Gaudí to create a new Episcopal seat right next to the cathedral, above the wall. The relationship between the bishop and the architect was formed years earlier, when Grau was General Vicar of the Archdiocese of Tarragona. The bishop inaugurated the chapel of the College of Jesus and Mary in Reus, where Gaudí had designed the alabaster altar and where his sick niece, Rosita Egea, was hospitalized.

During the construction of the Astorga palace, the two men had long conversations about liturgical reforms. Gaudí later based his designs for the Sagrada Família and for the reform of the Cathedral of Palma on these ideas.

At the beginning of the project, Gaudí was immersed in the construction of Güell Palace and in the plans for the Sagrada Família. He therefore asked the bishop to send him photographs, drawings, and information about the setting so that he could design a building in harmony with the surrounding architecture. The first proposals that Gaudí sent delighted Grau, but they did not convince the architecture section of the Academy of San Fernando in Madrid, which oversaw all ecclesiastical projects. After various modifications, the committee approved Gaudí's project, even though there was a heated debate over his design. After Grau's death, Gaudí abandoned the Astorga project.

*Gaudí completed the liturgical restoration in this large building made of granite from Bierzo*

Following the theories of Viollet-le-Duc, Gaudí constructed a building reminiscent of a medieval fortification, with numerous Gothic details.

The building was surrounded by a moat to facilitate ventilation and to illuminate the basement. The ground floor contains the kitchen, the secretary's office, the conference room, and the office of the court. The first floor accommodates the library, the bishop's office, the chapel, and the guest rooms. The rest of the bedrooms are located on the upper levels.

For the entrance, Gaudí envisioned a large foyer that would rise up to the roof. Skylights would distribute light to all of the floors. However, the architect who succeeded Gaudí, Ricardo García Guereta, disregarded this solution and constructed a totally blind roof, which hindered light from shining throughout the building.

On the façades, Gaudí used granite from Bierzo. Its light color has a symbolic function because it blends with the clergy's clothing. The nerves of the pointed arches on the façade are decorated with glazed ceramic pieces made in the neighboring village, Jiménez de Jamuz.

Photographs of Palacio Episcopal de Astorga: Roger Casas

Gaudí carefully studied local monuments before beginning the project. Since the palace is located between the Roman wall and the Gothic-Renaissance Cathedral, one of the architect's main objectives was to respect the surroundings.

As with the Crypt of the Sagrada Família, the architect surrounded the palace with a moat that provides ventilation for the basement spaces. This mechanism gives the property a feeling of strength. The portico of the main door has three large, trumpeted arches that were planned once construction had begun since they do not appear in the initial drawings. The angel bearer of the support is made of zinc and was manufactured by the Asturian Royal Company of Minas.

The cylindrical shaft columns that support the pointed arches are austere. Their capitals are adorned with subtle floral motifs and their bases are made of simple geometric forms that combine hexagons, small circles, and flat polyhedrons.

The pointed arches on the palace's ground floor are covered with small, dark red varnished ceramic pieces. The architect designed the templates and assigned Jiménez de Jamuz to create the ornaments. Gaudí did not design the floral engravings.

*Gaudí's work on the Cathedral of Palma de Mallorca and the Sagrada Família were based on the architect's long conversations with his friend, the Bishop of Astorga*

© Luis Gueilburt

# colegio de las teresianas

Ganduxer, 85, Barcelona
1888-1889

*"We didn't change, the more time we spent reflecting on new forms of architecture, the more certainty we had for the need to use them"*

everal conditions strongly influenced the design of this Theresian school located in the Sant Gervasi neighborhood of Barcelona. For one, this Carmelite community follows the rule of poverty. The building is also dedicated to the founder of the order, Saint Theresa, and adheres to a philosophy of life in agreement with the postulates of the Middle Age.

Another architect oversaw the initial works of the site, including the beginning of the construction of a complex with three buildings. When Gaudí took over in March 1889, the first and second floors of the building had already been determined.

Gaudí stayed within the budget for the project, which was limited in comparison to the funds he had for other commissions. He also followed the guidelines put in place by the previous architect, which meant that certain stretches could not be modified. His design respected the austerity, asceticism and sobriety that this ecclesiastical order required. Without abandoning his original and imaginative style, Gaudí exercised restraint and designed a building with striking yet contained elements. Though moderation is absent in his previous works, here it plays the starring role, at least in the forms, since —deep down— the building is full of symbolic elements.

For the exterior façade of this religious fortress designated for to the education of girls and the formation of religious people, Gaudí designed a rigorous volume of stone and brick which includes some ceramic, ornamental elements. The rectitude and rigidity of the

*Inspired by the symbolism of the seven levels of the ascension of Saint Theresa of Jesus, Gaudí designed this construction whose forceful and pointed profile projects between the adjacent buildings*

façade is broken by pointed arches of different sizes that cover the upper floor, as well as a projecting gallery. The building is rectangular and elongated, and a grand longitudinal axis organizes the interior space. The floor plan is divided into three parallel bands.

In the basement, an elongated corridor extends along the central zone, occupied on the ground floor by two large interior patios that distribute the natural light. Gaudí found heavy transversal support walls on the ground floor. He substituted them, using parabolic arches, with symmetrical, elongated hallways on the upper levels. This constructional solution eliminated the wall as a supporting element and created a dynamic composition. The arches, painted white to accentuate luminosity, are separated by windows that open onto the interior patios. The result is a tranquil atmosphere bathed in a soft, indirect light.

During the Civil War, the building suffered from various attacks, lootings and fires that destroyed some elements and decorative details that have never been replaced. In 1969, the building was declared an Historical–Artistic Monument of National Interest.

© Roger Casas

The conception of this work, like many before it, is enormously organic and shows a clear Gothic inspiration. This is demonstrated by the wrought iron work of the entrance door, which is repeated in some windows on the ground floor and on the third floor, as well as on the blinds and in the interior of the construction.

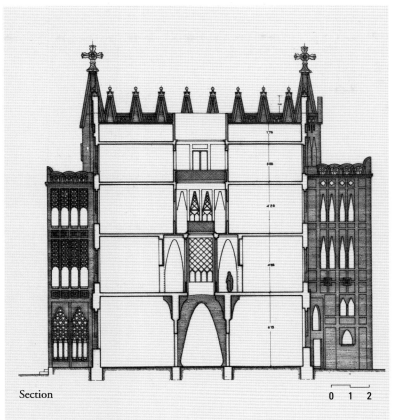

Section

0 1 2

# casa de los botines

Plaza de San Marcelo, León
1892-1893

*It was a challenge for Gaudí to create a neo–Gothic work in the center of León, near the splendid cathedral. His project surpassed all expectations and respected the environment*

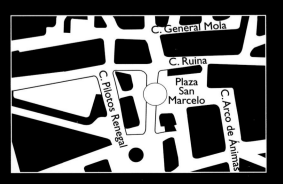

While Gaudí was finishing the construction of the Palacio Episcopal de Astorga, his friend and patron, Eusebi Güell recommended him to build a house in the center of León. Simón Fernández and Mariano Andrés, the owners of a company that bought fabrics from Güell, commissioned Gaudí to build a residential building with a warehouse. The nickname of the house comes from the last name of the company's former owner, Joan Homs i Botinàs.

With Casa de los Botines, the architect wanted to pay tribute to León's emblematic buildings. Therefore, he designed a building with a medieval air and numerous neo-Gothic characteristics. The building consists of four floors, a basement and an attic. Gaudí chose an inclined roof and placed towers in the corners to reinforce the project's neo-Gothic feel. To ventilate and illuminate the basement, he created a moat around two of the façades, a strategy that he would repeat in the Sagrada Família.

Gaudí placed the owners' dwellings on the first floor. These are accessed, respectively, by independent doors in the lateral and back façades. The upper floors house rental property and the lower floor contains the company offices. The principal door is crowned by a wrought iron inscription with the name of the company and by a great sculpture by San Jorge. During the restoration of the building in 1950, workers discovered a tube of lead under the sculpture containing the original plans signed by Gaudí and press clippings from the era.

*Casa de los Botines is the only project that Gaudí actually finished*

The foundations of Casa de los Botines were a subject of debate during the building's construction. Gaudí had envisioned a continuous base, like that of the city's cathedral. However, local technicians insisted on constructing on piles to make the floor, located at a great depth, more resistant. Despite rumors that the building would collapse during construction, the house has never had structural problems. On the ground floor, the architect used —for the first time— a system of cast iron pillars that leave the space free, without the need for the load-bearing walls to distribute it. Unlike Gaudí's previous projects, the façades of Casa de los Botines have a structural function.

On the inclined roof, six skylights supported by iron tie-beams illuminate and ventilate the attic. The ensemble is supported on a complex wooden framework.

In 1929, the savings bank of León bought the building and adapted it to its needs, without altering Gaudí's original project.

Photographs of Casa de los Botines: Roger Casas

In the corners of the house, Gaudí placed cylindrical towers topped with a column, which is doubled in the northern part to indicate the direction. Gaudí liked to show the cardinal points in his buildings and did so in Palau Güell, in Bellesguard, in Park Güell, and in Casa Batlló.

*This building has a neo-Gothic air and is made of stone, with angular towers. Surrounded by a moat, it is covered by a framework of wood and slate.*

EXPOSICIÓN
La Catedral de León, el Sueño de la Razón
1901 2001
OCTUBRE 2001   Caja España

The railings of the entrance were manufactured in Barcelona and crowned with a inscription of the names of the owners that was eventually replaced by the names of the new residents. The railings of the moat resemble those of Casa Vicens, since Gaudí used similar techniques and rivets.

The interior, which has been fully reformed over the years, still conserves some of the elements designed by Gaudí, including the magnificent marquetry work in the doors and windows and wrought iron elements such as the banisters and railings. In some rooms, one can contemplate the original structure made of a system of metal pillars with shafts and stone capitals.

The fascinating structure of the towers includes a framework of wooden strips with a helical form that are held up by vertical posts. Despite the irregularity of the pieces, the system is stable and has never required restoration.

# bodegas güell

Carretera C-246, Garraf, Barcelona
1895

*The bodegas are located on the land for which Gaudí had originally designed a hunting pavilion. Eusebi Güell requested the pavilion, but it was never built*

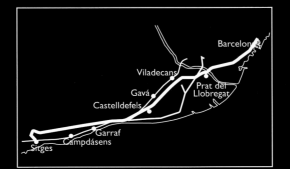

For many years, it was believed that the Bodegas Güell were designed by Francesc Berenguer i Mestres. However, the plans were not in the architect's archives and other factors led to the conclusion that Eusebi Güell had once again entrusted Gaudí to execute this project on one of his estates.

The land is located on the coasts of Garraf, to the south of Barcelona. At first, the client envisioned a hunting pavilion, in a similar style to Casa Vincens. He later rejected the idea and decided instead to build a bodega. Güell dedicated the surrounding terrain to the cultivation of vineyards, which produced a wine that was later served, for example, on the ships of the Transatlantic Company. The land was first leveled to even out the precipitous cliffs.

The development includes two buildings, an entrance pavilion and the bodegas. The In front of the buildings is a large iron door formed by a crossbeam of wrought iron with thick chains hanging from it. This combination of materials was not structurally necessary but Gaudí decorated some façades in this way in order to avoid simplicity. A grand arch crowned by a balcony mirador receives visitors and contains the door of the concierge's house.

The bodegas are located in an austere and striking building, evocative of military architecture and made of stone extracted from nearby quarries. The roof has two inclinations, one of which reaches the ground and becomes part of the façade. Experts say the architect was inspired by oriental pagodas. The chimneys are typical of Gaudí and reveal his surprising imagination.

*The bodegas rise up forcefully in a unique setting that the architect respected by using local materials*

The cellars are located on the ground floor. The first floor contains the residence, and the attic accommodates a chapel, which explains the appearance of a belfry on the roof.

From a formal point of view, Bodegas Güell looks nothing like other buildings that Gaudí had, or would, design. However, the genius never repeated himself. His designs were a constant innovation in the fields of structure, composition and construction. Therefore, it is not unusual that the resources used here were not repeated in other projects.

© Pere Planells

© Pere Planells

Though this work does not feature characteristic elements of Gaudí, his style is obvious in the parabolic arches, in the masterly use of exposed construction and in the wrought iron door of the entrance.

© Pere Planells

The building is located near the cave of the Falconer, where a large, underground river flows into the sea. Güell wanted to divert the river towards Barcelona. On the grounds, there is also a medieval watchtower that is connected to the residence via a bridge.

The large roof that transforms into the façade emphasizes Gaudí's wish to link all the constructional elements of his works. The roof serves as an umbrella and a parasol for the building and has structural functions.

# casa calvet

## Casp, 48, Barcelona
### 1898-1900

*"When the plasterers had to begin the ceilings, which were very ornate, they went on strike; so that the project would not be stalled and to teach them a lesson, I decided to substitute the level ceilings for simple, thin coffered ceilings"*

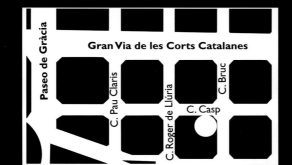

When Barcelona's City Hall decided in 1900 to give an award for the best building of the year, officials chose the construction that Gaudí had designed for D. Pedro Martir Calvet. A textile manufacturer, Calvet assigned the building to the architect in 1898. The award was the only recognition Gaudí received during his lifetime for a project.

Casa Calvet was Gaudí's first attempt at residential housing design. Until the assignment, Gaudí had never designed a residential building, and the concept —quite different from his usual commissions— was a challenge for him.

The Calvet building is located between other buildings on a street in Barcelona's Eixample neighborhood. The distribution of this zone and builders's attempt to make the most of the land gave Eixample buildings a standard style. As a result, Casa Calvet is one of Gaudí's most conventional constructions, since he had to repress the tremendous display of imagination and genius shown in his other works. Nevertheless, the building is a clear demonstration of how it is possible to design personalized constructions despite limitations and determined architectural possibilities.

The ground floor of the property was reserved for a warehouse, an office (this space is now occupied by a restaurant that conserves some decorative elements from the era) and the main floor. The rest of the building was designated for rental housing. To give the building his personal touch, Gaudí designed each one of the apartments in a different manner.

The main façade displays more restrained forms than the back façade, where Gaudí developed a more personal and ambitious work. Made of carved stone, the façade's apparent austerity does little to warn of the creative foyer behind it. The extraordinary masonry work gives the building a rough aspect and a unique relief, softened by the lobed, wrought iron balconies and diverse sculptural elements.

*For this building of rental apartments, Gaudí dared to freely interpret Neo-baroque, combining it with other, more personal styles*

The architect gave special importance to the interior decoration of the residences. He designed some of the office furnishings, including an easy chair with arms for one and two places, a table and a chair. This collection was his first foray into this area of design.

© Pere Planells

© Pere Planells

Elevation and section

0 1 2

© Roger Casas

© Joana Furió

© Joana Furió

Over the entrance door –placed exactly in the center of the main façade– is a small, lavishly decorated lookout-platform. On the lower part is a crest of Catalonia, the owner's initial and the image of a cypress. These are examples of symbolic references that would later have significance in the Sagrada Família.

For the construction of this house, Gaudí opted to make a plaster model of the façade. He presented this solution –more practical, schematic, and detailed than blueprints– to City Hall. The consortium selected the building, by majority not unanimously, as the best of the year. The ground floor now houses a restaurant that conserves some of the original decorative elements.

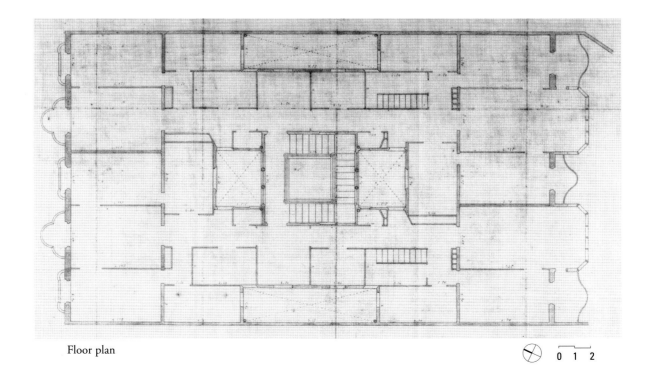

Detail of a balcony

Floor plan

0 1 2

# crypt of the colonia güell

Reixac, s/n, Santa Coloma de Cervelló, Barcelona
1908-1916

*"One must not want to be original, because style itself comes from within and comes out spontaneously"*

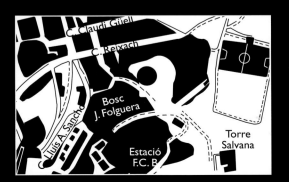

The Colonia Güell is one of Gaudí's most original and interesting works, even though the project was never completed. Gaudí had free reign to design the colony and spent almost ten years studying the plans. Construction began in 1908, but he was only able to build the crypt of the church. When Count Güell died in 1914, the project was abandoned.

The assignment entailed building a housing development for a small settlement of workers next to Eusebi Güell´s textile factory in Santa Coloma de Cervelló, located 20 kilometers from Barcelona, in Baix Llobregat. The colony was to occupy 30 hectares of a 160-hectare estate. The workers's residences were designed to surround the factory and Güell had planned to construct all types of facilities for the residents, including a church. An inspired Gaudí designed a complex settlement with constant references to nature. For example, the church, situated on a small hill, would have blended in with its natural surroundings. Gaudí's plan was to use organic forms and a studied polychromy so that the dark tones of the bricks of the crypt would merge with the tree trunks. The green tone of the church walls would have fused with the trees, and the high ceilings of the church would have transformed into blue and white in order to blend with the sky and the clouds. For Gaudí, this special chromatic plan represented nature and symbolized, at a deeper level, the path of the Christian life.

*An example of mystic architecture. Though this project was never finished, Gaudí created a new method of calculating structures based on a model constructed with cables that held small sacks full of pellets*

Gaudí's design took advantage of the land's pronounced slope to include a crypt with a portico and a chapel, reached through steps on the portico. The crypt is a complex and perfect skeleton made out of brick, stone and blocks of basalt. Its floor plan has the shape of a star, made possible by the inclination of the exterior walls. Since the crypt is covered by a vault walled up with long, thin bricks on ribs of brick, it looks like the shell of a tortoise from the exterior. Inside, it appears more like the enormous twisted skeleton of a snake. Four inclined columns of basalt situated at the entry invite visitors to enter.

Photographs of the Crypt of the Colonia Güell: Pere Planells

Inside the crypt, basalt pillars would have been the principal support of the church if it had been built. Their solidity contrasts with the delicateness of the multi-colored stained glass windows.

Sketch of the crypt

*Gaudí's religions architecture combined construction and liturgy with other disciplines ranging from music to philosophy*

The large, different circular openings in resplendent colors that perforate the walls of the crypt allow exterior light to enter, creating a spectacular play of light and shadow.

# bellesguard

Bellesguard, 16-20, Barcelona
1900-1909

*Bellesguard is built on the same terrain on which King Martí l'Humà I constructed a retreat. The property has a view of the sea and the king could watch the galleys arrive. The estate is Gaudí's most significant tribute to Catalonia's great medieval past.*

The country house of María Sagués, widow of Jaume Figueras and a fervent admirer of Gaudí, was constructed on land that, in the 15th century, was the site of the summer residence of the last Catalan king, Martí I ("The Human"). In fact, the name of the estate, "Bell Esguard," means "beautiful view" and dates to this era. It refers to the estate's striking location and a splendid view of the city of Barcelona.

When Gaudí accepted the commission to design María Sagués' home, few traces remained of what was formerly the medieval mansion of a king. Nevertheless, Gaudí´s design could be considered a type of tribute to the architecture of Catalonia´s medieval past. Gaudí conserved the ruins of the mansion and offered his own personal version of different historical and stylistic concepts. His architectural genius is evident in both the striking and solemn volumes that make up the façade and in the house's interior.

The exterior of this noble building, covered with stone, is vaguely reminiscent of medieval constructions and adapts perfectly to its surroundings. The various windows that perforate the walls of the façade are lobed arches in the Gothic style. The svelte tower situated at one of the extremes features one of the architect's most characteristic touches: the four-pointed cross.

Bellesguard is a residence with a simple, nearly square floor plan. The four principal diagonals are oriented towards the cardinal points. The house has a semi-basement, a ground floor, an apartment and an attic.

Covered vaults with low profiles supported by cylindrical pillars define the structure of the semi-basement, giving it a rough, almost monastic, aspect. On the upper level, the brick vaults turn into a more decorative element by exposing the color of the brick. In this space, great luminosity is achieved thanks, in part, to the ample openings. On the upper floors, Gaudí created diaphanous and open spaces by adding numerous windows and by recovering the walls with plaster. These solutions managed to accentuate the luminosity —difficult to perceive from the outside— while creating attractive plays of light and shadow. The roof of the attic is supported by a structure formed by mushroom-shaped capitals made of projecting brick.

*By going up to the Three Crosses of Park Güell and situating himself next to the main cross, he had of view of the cross that presides over Bellesguard*

© Miquel Tres

© Miquel Tres

Crowning the svelte and high tower of the building are the four-pointed cross, the royal crown and the four bars of the Catalan-Aragonese flag. All of these elements are represented helically in stone and are covered with "trencadís."

© Joana Furió

© Joana Furió

Contrasting textures are habitual in the work of the Catalan architect and Bellesguard is no exception. Gaudí covered some windows with grates; in this case, round iron bars. The grates are a decorative element that also providence protection.

At Bellesguard, Gaudí combined wrought iron with stained glass windows in a masterly and precise way. Of particular interest is the lamp in the foyer. Gaudí played with triangles to make up the lamp's structure and with circles to adorn the glass. The architect's close collaboration with specialized artisans was of utmost importance when it came to creating the decorative elements of his buildings.

The mosaics found in different spaces of the building are more than just decorative elements and should be interpreted as symbolic references. The mosaics are a reminder of historic eras during which Catalonia enjoyed great political and economic splendor.

# park güell

### Olot, s/n, Barcelona
#### 1900-1914

*With genius and determination, Gaudí designed the park as a residential city. What was meant to be a residential paradise in the middle of the city eventually became an urban park enjoyed by all of Barcelona.*

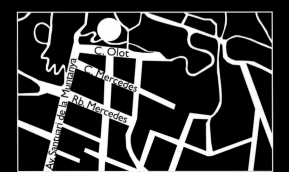

usebi Güell was an admirer of English landscape gardening. Envisioning a new model of the English "garden-city," he decided to develop some land known as the "Bald Mountain" in the neighborhood of Gràcia. Güell entrusted the project to his friend and protégé Antoni Gaudí. His goal was to create a residential space close to the city that would attract the wealthy Catalan bourgeoisie. Unfortunately, the project was unsuccessful, and the terrain was converted into a public park in 1922, when Barcelona's City Hall bought the land from Güell's heirs.

Gaudí designed the complex as a housing development protected and isolated by a surrounding wall. With seven gates, the wall features undulating lines and is made of rubblework, with inlaid "trencadís" ceramics, a mosaic made of broken pieces of tile. This ornamentation is repeated in numerous compositional elements. Park

*Park Güell is the result of Gaudí's respect for the land and nature, his profound knowledge of construction know-how and his unlimited imagination*

Güell occupies two properties: Can Coll i Pujol and Can Muntaner de Dalt, which were divided into 60 parcels. The plots had a triangular form adapted to the topography of the land, full of uneven stretches and slopes. Only three of the plots were sold: the Trias family bought two and Gaudí purchased the one used as a model, where he lived until he moved to the Sagrada Família. His former residence now houses the Gaudí museum.

Inside, two pavilions flank the wrought iron gate of the entrance door. The one situated on the left was designated for services and the one on the right contained the residence of the concierge. Both pavilions have an oval floor plan and are remarkable for their architectural structure, based on reinforced ceramic tie-beams and small brick vaults supported by load-bearing walls. There is a notable absence of right angles. In front of this entrance, a grand double staircase with symmetrical flights of stairs leads to the Column Room, formed by 86 classic columns. The stairs then lead to the Greek theatre, a grand esplanade situated above that is bordered by a continual bench with wavy lines. The flights of stairs are separated by small islands with organic decorative elements. The first takes the form of a cave, the second features a reptile head projecting out of a medallion with the Catalan flag, and the third presents the multicolored figure of a dragon. In 1969, Park Güell was named an Historical – Artistic Monument of National Interest. In 1984, UNESCO declared the park a World Heritage site.

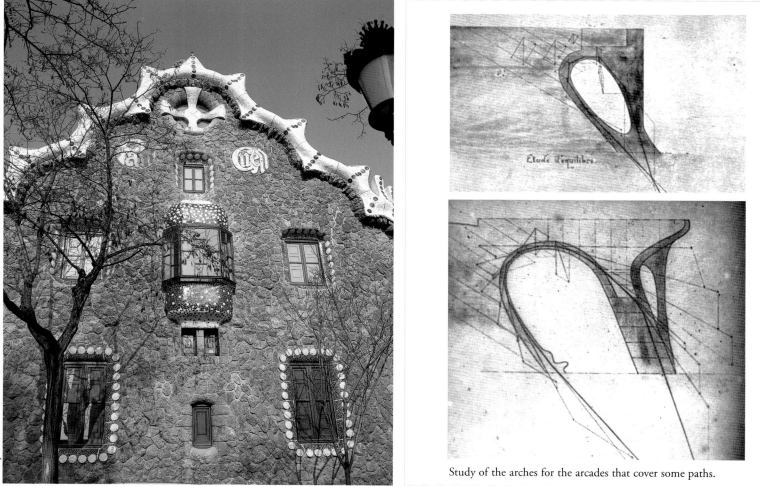

Étude l'équilibre.

Study of the arches for the arcades that cover some paths.

The pavilions that flank the door of the main entrance appear like something out of a fairy tale and entice the visitor to enter a magical world. The pavilions are made of stone –as is the wall that surrounds the property– and are covered with multi-colored ceramic pieces. Though it doesn't seem so at first, the two buildings are perfectly integrated with the rest of Gaudí's composition.

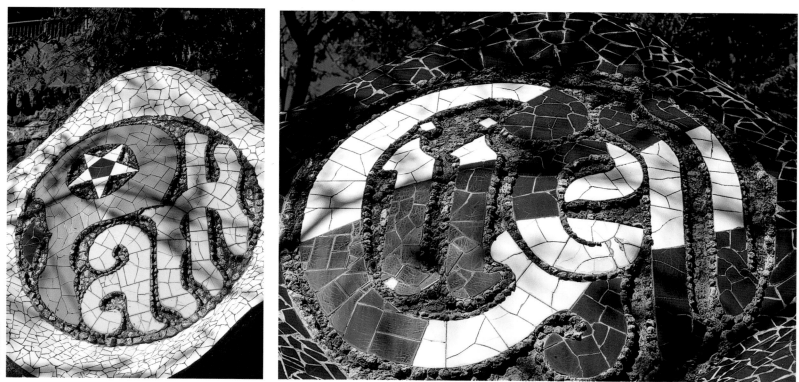

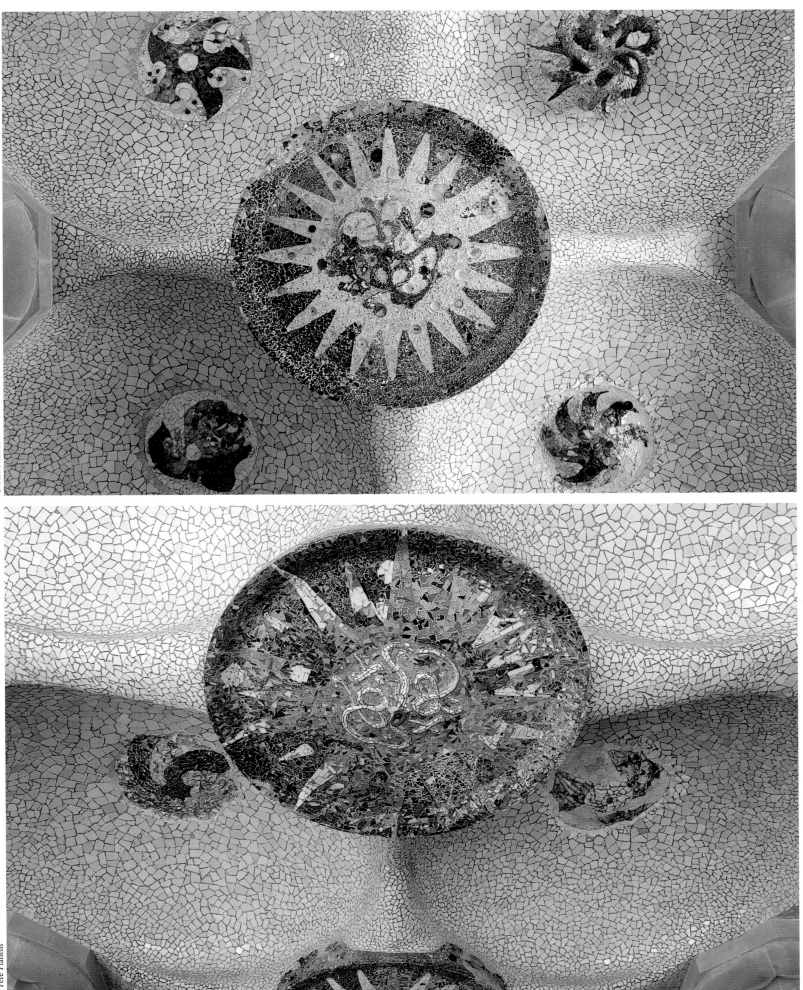

© Miquel Tres

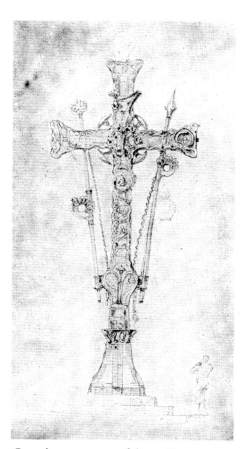

Cross that crowns one of the pavilions

*Only on rare occasions has an architect managed to combine so brilliantly urbanism, architecture and nature. Gaudí meticulously and skillfully created a fascinating space full of symbolism*

Sketch of the entrance pavilion

© Pere Planells

© Pere Planells

© Pere Planells

© Pere Planells

Stone is used in many spaces of the park to create forms similar to those found in nature. Stone's solidity and austerity contrasts with the richness and chromatic diversity of "trencadís" which is used on the long, undulating bench situated on the esplanade overlooking the city, above the Column Room. Mosaic medallions adorn the Column Room's ceiling, the roof of the two pavilions, the steps and the entrance fountain.

# finca miralles

Paseo Manuel Girona, 55, Barcelona
1901-1902

*The undulating walls take on a life of their own, like a serpent
that guards the estate*

While Gaudí was immersed in his first grand residential project, Casa Calvet, he accepted another, smaller assignment. His friend Hermenegild Miralles Anglès asked him to design a door and a surrounding wall for his estate on the old private road of Eusebi Güell. Today, the road is a busy avenue between the neighborhoods of Les Corts and Sarrià. Even though some experts claim Gaudí drew the plans for the house and the cottage that were later built on the estate, the architect Domènech Sugrañes has found no evidence to support the premise.

The close friendship between the architect and the client led them to collaborate in various activities. Aside from being a printer, a bookbinder and an editor, Hermenegild Miralles manufactured all types of things, from toys to decorative tiles, which Gaudí used in some of his projects, like the Vincens house or the Torino bar. Gaudí also used Miralles's powerful hydraulic press to create resistance trials to test the pillars of his projects.

The wall that Gaudí designed to surround the estate is wavy. Structurally, this meant that it needed more thickness in the base and a slimmer section in the upper part. For materials, Gaudí used ceramic bricks and the remains of Arabic tiles together with lime mortar. He crowned the wall with a continual element that winds above it.

The door that he created for the carriages entrance has an irregular, arched form. The wall opens to create access to the forms which fold through various curves. A helical interior framework of variable thickness supports the door that seems to stand thanks to magic, since there is no external element that absorbs the eccentric loads.

*The roof that crowns the door conceals the boundless imagination demonstrated by the property*

A canopy completes the door's wavy forms. The canopy is formed by tie-beams built into the door, which are supported by fibercement tiles and helical braces. This element was eliminated in 1965 for exceeding municipal ordinances and was replaced by a smaller one in 1977.

To the right of the grand entrance is a small iron door through which pedestrians enter. The effort made to shape the metal is noteworthy since it bends at its slimmest part. Between the two doors a large column rises up where Gaudí had planned to place a Catalan coat of arms and an inscription with the name of the owner. However, this plan was never accomplished.

Photographs of Finca Miralles: Roger Casas

The project is located near the door of the dragon of the Güell estate. Both projects feature exceptional ironwork, though the forms of the door to the Miralles estate –made up of a system of bars hung in various ways– are more austere. Right next to the door is a large medallion that was supposed to contain the owner's initials and a crest of Catalonia.

# restoration of the cathedral in palma de mallorca

Plaza Almoina, Palma de Mallorca
1903-1914

*Gaudí did not treat religion in a passive way; instead, his boundless creativity inspired him to reinterpret liturgical spaces*

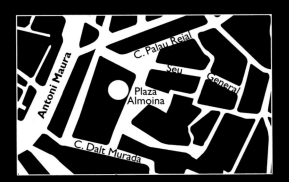

The bishop Pere Campins i Barceló met Gaudí in 1889, during the construction of the Sagrada Família. Campins was fascinated by Gaudí's artistic and architectural talent and was highly impressed by his knowledge of the Catholic liturgy, which the architect developed during his conversations with the bishop of Astorga. Years later, the Cathedral Chapter approved Campins's proposal to restore the cathedral in Palma, which is regarded as one of the most beautiful examples of Catalan Gothic architecture. Without hesitation, the bishop assigned the project to Gaudí.

The architect's ambitious design aimed to emphasize the building's Gothic character. On one hand, Gaudí changed the site of some elements: he moved the choir of the nave to the presbytery and the small back chorus to a side chapel. He also obtained permission to move the baroque altar in order to expose the old Gothic one. This left the Episcopal chair and the Trinidad chapel in full view. On the other hand, Gaudí designed new pieces to embellish and amplify the space, including the railings, lights and liturgical furnishings. He also reinforced the structure, having perceived a slight sagging of the columns, on which he hung some forged rings that support lights.

The relocation of elements made the altar the centerpiece, for which Gaudí designed an octagonal baldachin with symbolic references. The seven corners allude to the seven virtues of the Saint Spirit and the 50 small lamps make reference to the celebration of the Pentecost. He also added sculptures of Christ, Mary and Saint John in the stone cross as an allusion to the Divine Redemption. He considered introducing other groups of sculptures, but abandoned the idea before construction had begun.

*Due to various reforms, the house had an eclectic style that included influences from Central European architecture and traces of Moorish features*

Gaudí designed nine stained glass windows, a rose window and seven large windows, dedicated to Regina of the litany. However, only some of them were hung in the cathedral. The last one he designed is conserved intact in the vestry.

Gaudí's project included the restoration of the building, as well as reforms in some of the liturgical aspects carried out in the cathedral. For the most conservative, Gaudí's intervention deviated too much from the rules and the congregation complained to the clergy. Gaudí left the work unfinished and moved on to concentrate on the Sagrada Família, where he felt no restrictions on his creative efforts.

Photographs and drawings of the Cathedral in Palma: Gabriel Vicens

© Pere Planells

While Gaudí's reorganization of the interior was limited to a certain space, his numerous ironwork designs are found throughout the cathedral, including on the exterior. Of particular interest are the doors and railings formed by united circles and supported by spherical banisters.

*Gaudí's intervention in the Cathedral of Palma de Mallorca complied with the ideals of an ecclesiastical reform that found it imperative to adapt the liturgy to the era's evolution of thought, which was slightly out of date*

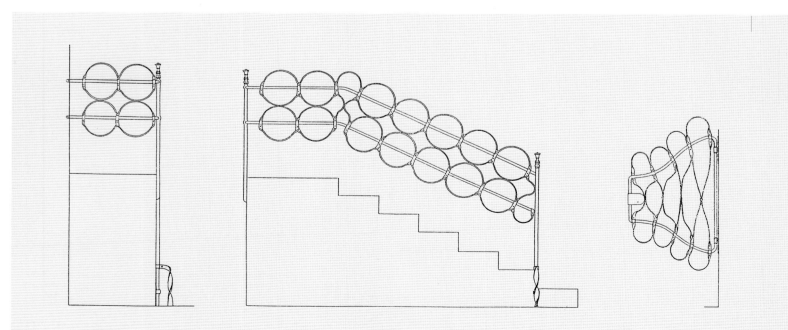

Door and railing of the Corpus Christi gallery.

Stairway of the exhibition of the Holy Sacrament in the Chapel of the Pietà.

Gaudí's unmistakable designs are apparent in even the smallest details of the cathedral, such as the delicate wooden benches painted an old gold color or the ornaments displayed in the confessional.

The rings that hold up the columns of the central nave are situated 16 feet above ground and support candles with small trays that catch the wax. The structural system is comprised of pieces inserted in the stone, and rivets support the candelabras.

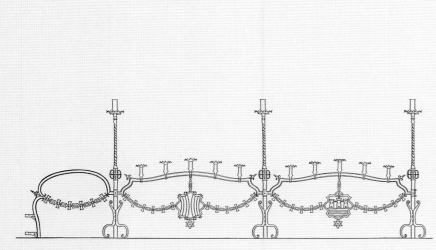

Railing of the presbytery

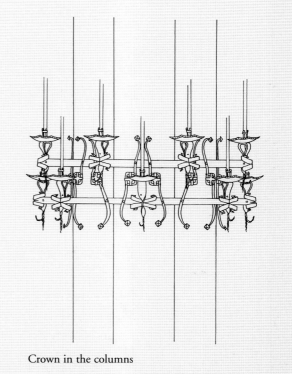

Crown in the columns

© Pere Planells

# casa batlló

Passeig de Gràcia, 43, Barcelona
1904-1906

*The polychromy of the stone, the ceramic pieces and the stained glass windows are a metaphor of a rural vision: under the bruise color of the mountains are all the luminous shades of morning dew.*

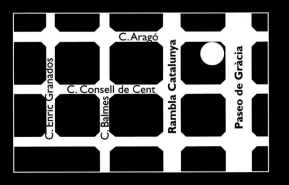

Casa Batlló is located between the Ametller house, by Modernist architect Puig i Cadalfalch, and a traditional building of the Eixample neighborhood, designed by Emili Sala. The building was constructed in 1877 and its owner, the textile manufacturer Josep Batlló i Casanovas, commissioned Gaudí to remodel the façade and to redistribute the courtyards. When Pere Milà, a friend of the industrialist, heard of Batlló's intention to update his house's image, he immediately presented him to Gaudí, of whom he was a fervent admirer. Even though the project meant working on an existing building, Gaudí gave the project his personal touch and the Batlló house became one of the most emblematic projects of his extensive career.

The exterior of the building demonstrates Gaudí's compositional sensitivity. The first floor is covered with stones from Marés and glass, while ceramic disks shroud the upper floors. During the renovation, the architect stood on the street and decided the optimal position of each piece so that they would stand out and shine with force. The workers put them up gradually, according to Gaudí's instructions. This manner of working-improving and perfecting an initial idea during the construction process-is repeated in all of Gaudí's works and reflects his dedication to his projects, which were almost never labeled finished. This method caused some bureaucratic problems, since the authorities need-

*When the first rays of morning light shine on the façade of Casa Batlló, there is an iridescent effect and various plays of light*

ed, and need, to approve finished projects. To avoid conflicts, Gaudí sketched the plans of his projects, allowing for their evolution during construction.

The poetry of the façade culminates in the roof, which is topped with pinkish-blue ceramic pieces in the form of scales. A final point, with a base of spherical and cylindrical pieces, evokes the back of a dragon. A tower crowned by a small, convex cross tops the building. However, despite Casa Batlló's surprising and innovative geometry and colors, Gaudí kept its location in mind and adapted its height to that of the neighboring buildings. The chimneys and water deposits on the roof are recovered with pieces of glass and colored tile on a mortar base.

In the entryway, an oak staircase leads up to the main floor. From this level, the staircase moves laterally towards the upper floors, which contain rental housing barely touched by Gaudí.

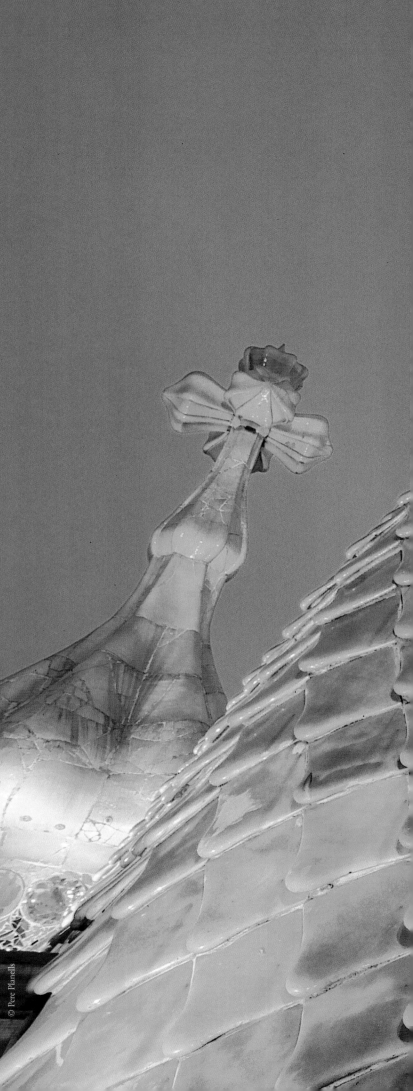

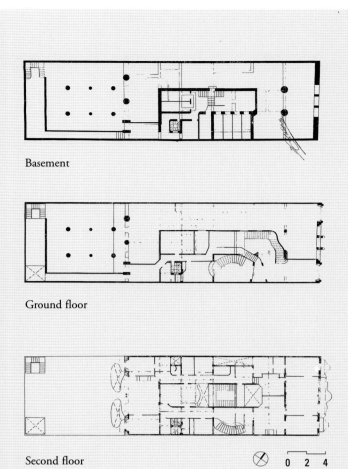

Basement

Ground floor

Second floor

⊗  0  2  4

The artist's boundless imagination is evident in the details of the screen that separates the room of the oratory, and in the door of the hall. The works of marquetry commissioned by Gaudí were created in the workshops of Casa & Bardés. The oratory, which is still owned by the Batlló family, includes distinct pieces, like the Sagrada Família by Josep Llimona.

© Miquel Tres

Throughout the building, one can appreciate the architect's desire to create continuous spaces, since there are no arris, corners or right angles. Partitions exist because of curvaceous transitions that evoke organic forms.

*The chimney of the hall is one of the practical devices used by Gaudí to endow the spaces with quality and comfort*

© Miquel Tres

© Pere Planells

The courtyard around which the staircase winds is covered with ceramic pieces. High up, they are ultramarine blue, and their color slowly softens until it becomes white on the ground floor. This chromatic degradation causes a uniform reflection of the light, creating similar tones throughout the height of the patio. From the caretaker's quarters, one sees a unique gray pearl color.

The façade of Casa Batlló is a phenomenal exercise of composition. On the lower part, Gaudí modeled the stone as if it were a clay sculpture. The front is complemented by slender pillars with vegetable motifs and stained glass windows with colors that create various luminous tonalities in the interior.

# casa milà

Passeig de Gràcia, 92, Barcelona
1906-1910

*It would not surprise me if, in the future, this house became a hotel, given the easy way to change the distributions and the abundance of bathrooms"*

The Milà house, located on one of the corners of the intersection between Passeig de Gràcia and the street Provenca, rises up like a large, rocky formation. Ever since its construction, Barceloneses have called it "La Pedrera" ("The Stone Quarry"). Pere Milà and his wife Roser Segimón assigned the house to Gaudí, and it was the architect's last civil project, since he later withdrew to the workroom of the Sagrada Família.

With this project, the artist wanted to make up for the lack of monuments in Barcelona, about which he often complained. His growing devotion to the Virgin Mary inspired a large building crowned by a bronze sculpture with the image of the Virgin, patron of the property. Even though he did not use the image in the end, La Pedrera still conserves some religious inscriptions.

Since the building had large dimensions, Gaudí devised a system of saving materials, so that the execution would be possible. He substituted load-bearing walls for a system of main beams and pillars. He carefully designed the links in order to reduce their section. He also envisioned a seemingly heavy and forceful façade, which, in reality, is formed by slim, limestone plaques from Garraf on the lower part and from Vilafranca on the upper levels. The quantity of iron used has caused more than one expert in structures to tremble.

The sinuous forms of the façade, so often compared to the swell of the sea, have their complement inside. In La Pedrera's interior, the right angle disappears, fixed partition walls are nonexistent, and every detail is drawn to the millimeter. A good example of Gaudí's careful design are the level ceilings, which create numerous forms out of plaster: the foam of the waves, the petals of a flower or the tentacles of an octopus. The architect's meticulous work is also evident in the wrought iron of the balconies, in the woodwork and in the hydraulic mosaics.

*"Vegetation is the means by which the earth becomes man's companion, his friend, his teacher"*

As in the Casa Batlló, Gaudí let his imagination run wild on the roof where the staircase boxes are extravagant volumes covered with small ceramic pieces. The helical forms of the chimneys emphasize the whirl of the smoke.

Even though Gaudí never finished the project because of a disagreement with the client, Casa Milà is one of the most complete examples of Gaudí architecture. The house displays intelligent constructional solutions, a striking compositional sensibility and an exuberant imagination.

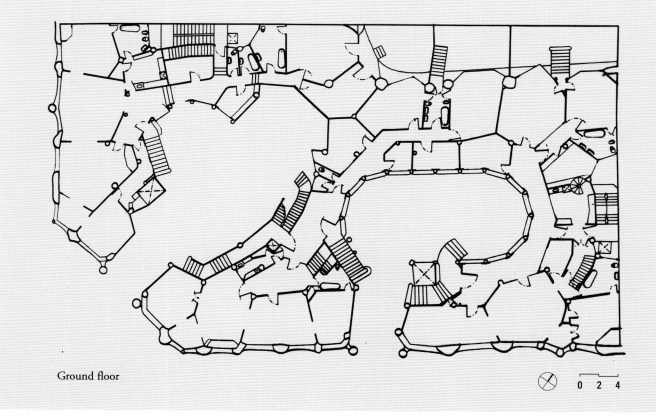

Ground floor

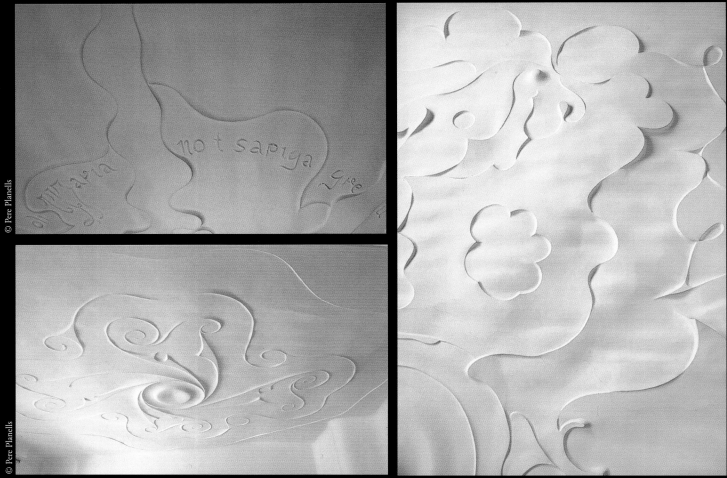

As with the façade, all the constructional elements of the interior have a sculptural character. A good example of this are the false ceilings which have no right angles. The forms that adorn the plaster finishes evoke the foam of waves and reproduce floral motifs and inscriptions, most of them religious.

© Pere Planells

The chimneys of the terrace roof rise up above the façade of Casa Milà, and pedestrians can admire them from the street Passeig de Gràcia. Some of the chimneys are covered with small, colored ceramic pieces and others with glass chips from champagne bottles.

© Joana Furió

© Pere Planells

# artigas gardens

La Pobla de Lillet, Lleida
1905

*Even though Gaudí used similar resources to those of Park Güell, here he included an element absent in other projects: water, which he used to create a fantastic, moist garden*

After an extensive study conducted by the Gaudí Real Cátedra, it was determined that Gaudí had in fact designed the gardens surrounding the old Artigas factory, in the province of Lleida. The architect received the assignment when he visited the prosperous industrialist, Joan Artigas i Alart, at his home in La Pobla de L´Illet.

The estate is located on the banks of the Llobregat river, near its source. This presented the architect with the opportunity to design the only humid garden he would create during his career. The site is elongated and follows the course of the river. A bridge marks the natural entrance to the property and leads the visitor to a cave and a spectacular natural fountain called La Magnèsia ("The Magnesia"), the name by which the project is widely known.

A winding path leads to the second bridge where Gaudí intervened by building a small cylindrical arbor surrounded by walls made of dry stone and covered with a pointed dome. Further along the

*The garden path follows the Llobregat river in its first stretch*

path, the visitor reaches the last bridge that Gaudí designed. The stones of this bridge are placed to resemble stalactite. One of the extremes transforms into a pergola that shelters visitors from inclement weather.

In order to trace and embellish the site's path along the river, Gaudí also added numerous flowerbeds and indigenous bushes. He put up small walls with little ceramic pieces and placed various sculptures around the park, including animal figures made of stone.

Even though Park Güell was designed on dry land, it shares certain similarities with the Artigas Gardens: the symbolism of the sculptures, the use of stone and wood, and the planting of species like yuccas, palm trees and rosebushes.

Photographs of Artigas Gardens: Miquel Tres

Even though the symbolism of the sculptures is repeated in all the projects of the genius architect, the figures of this work do not represent any story. They are only representations of animals and characters, and have nothing to do with mythology or religion.

unconstructed projects

# unconstructed projects

When the crypt of the Sagrada Família burned in 1936, much of the graphic documentation that the architect kept with him disappeared. However, Gaudí was not an architect who relied solely on plans; he also worked with models and preferred to make changes during the construction, as the project developed. The lack of information has led to many speculations about his creations. Almost a century later, we are still discovering new work by the brilliant architect. This book presents only some of the projects that he designed but never constructed. We feature some of the most important ones in this chapter.

The Marquis of Comillas commissioned Gaudí to design a building for Franciscan missionaries in the Moroccan city of Tangier. After a trip to the site in 1892, Gaudí began to draw the project, which he finished the following year.

In 1882, Gaudí designed a hunting pavilion for Eusebi Güell on an extensive property that Güell owned on the coasts of Garraf, to the south of Barcelona. The pavilion was never constructed. Instead, Gaudí built Bodegas Güell on the land, with the collaboration of Francesc Berenguer. The pavilion is reminiscent of the Vicens house and "El Capricho," two buildings that he designed during the same era.

In 1876, when Gaudí was still studying at Barcelona's Escuela Técnica Superior de Arquitectura, he designed the colonnade of a covered patio for the Council of Barcelona. The capitals and the arches are decorated with floral motifs that Gaudí repeated in many of his works.

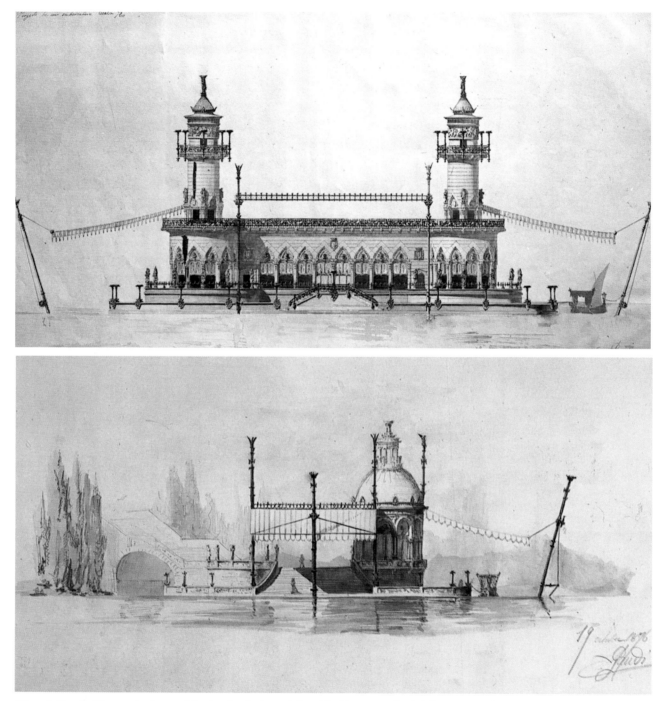

Though Gaudí did not win the special prize that he longed for with this project, he did demonstrate that, even as a student, his skill and imagination had no limits. The drawing's details and formal complexity reveal the young architect's talent.

n 1908, an American businessman, seduced by Gaudí's talent, commissioned him to design a large hotel in Manhattan. The architect envisioned an ambitious, 987-foot-high building that recalled the Sagrada Família. Only a few original drawings remain of the hotel.

details and furnishings

# stained glass windows

The possibility of manufacturing thicker glass in different colors encouraged the use of stained glass windows. As ornamentation, vegetable elements and polychromes dominate and manage to bathe the interiors with a variable and peculiar light.

Stained glass windows are an important element in Gaudi´s work. The windows reaffirm the Modernist effort to integrate the arts into the functional aspects of architecture and to recuperate artistic traditions that had faded over the years.

# chimneys

The diverse figures that cover the terrace roofs of buildings like the Pedrera or Palau Güell are enigmatic chimneys or ventilation tubes that once again demonstrate Gaudí's creative talent.

The chimneys are disguised by sculptural pieces that represent the image of medieval warriors. They are crowned with forms inspired by nature or covered with "trencadís" to break the chromatic monotony. Gaudí even applied his imagination to the areas that are out of sight, like the flat roofs.

# "trencadís"

Gaudí covered surfaces with fragments of multi-colored ceramics, a decorative technique called "trencadís." This solution, used for façades and different constructional details, is one of Gaudí's trademarks.

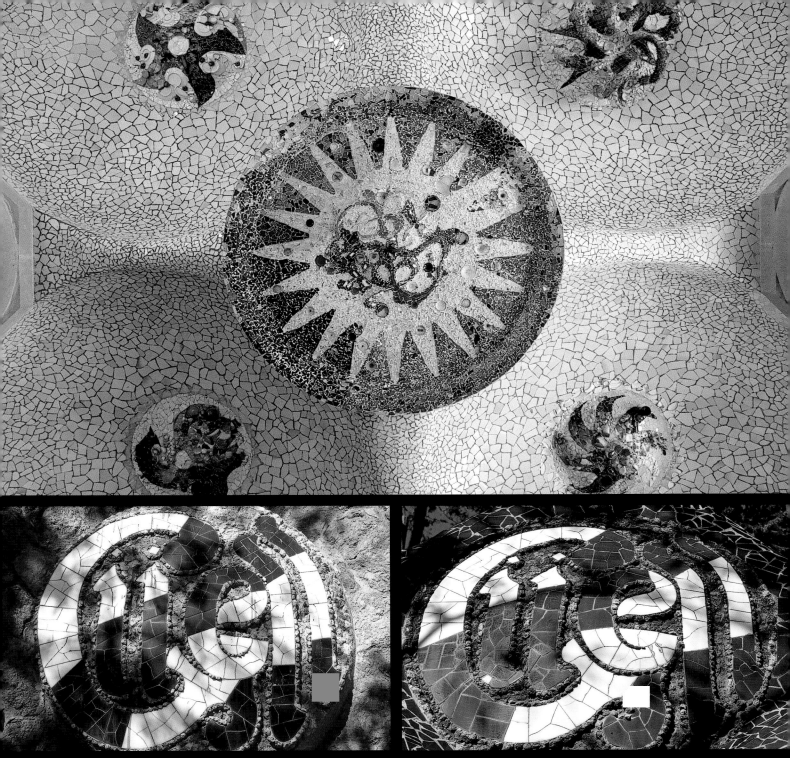

Gaudí revived the old Mediterranean tradition of using broken tiles to decorate architectural elements. The application of "trencadís" also kept construction costs low.

# ceramics

Gaudí resurrected the use of ceramics, another old decorative technique used in the Mediterranean zones. Gaudí managed to create surprising decorative images with tile, starting with daily and conventional elements.

Gaudí combined the influence of historic tradition with ornamental ideas from other cultures. The Oriental and Islamic cultures frequently inspired his decorative finishes in which ceramics, presented in a variety of forms, play an important role.

Gaudí chose to liberate forms from the restricted and cold academics that prevailed during his era. Common elements, like doors, are presented with expressivity and imagination, and are free of formal limitations.

During Gaudí's time, it was possible to develop any form, idea or color. This permitted him to fill his works with revolutionary concepts. Creative art formed part of the architect's buildings and was an expression of his personality.

# wrought iron

With the help of expert artisans, Gaudí molded iron at will and made this material - new in its day - take on expressive forms full of symbolism.

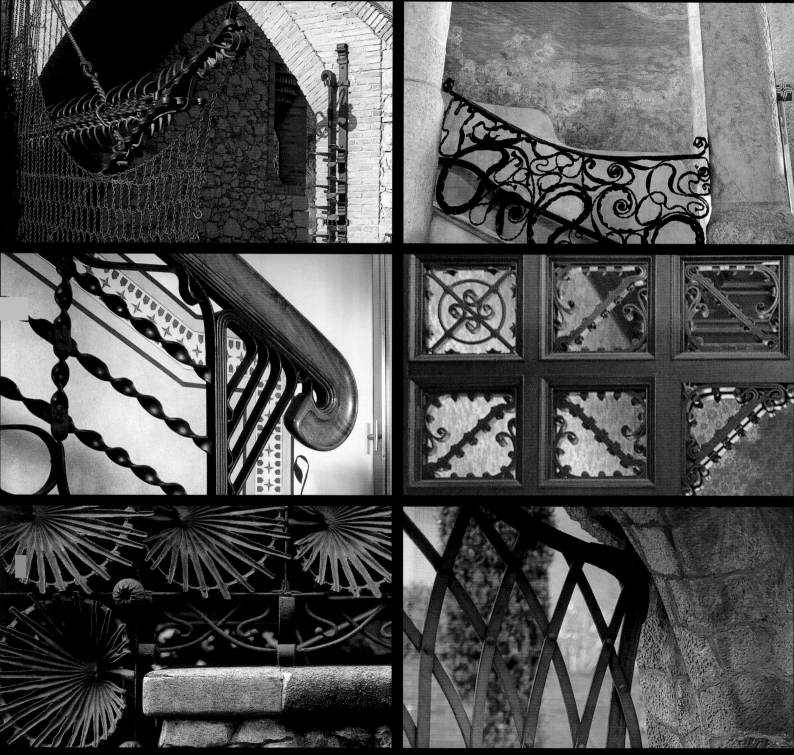

Railings, windows, grates, banisters, doors, balconies and benches.... all were susceptible to reinterpretation in wrought iron. Gaudí designed these elements for constructional purposes, but also for ornamentation.

# animals

Gaudí´s special creative universe included animal representations. Some of them were quite realistic, to the point of perfection. Others were born from fantasy, as animated beings that emerged from the artist's imagination.

The architect's language is one of art. His work is full of forms that represent animal forms. The use of animals in his architecture enlivens the constructions

# Natural motifs

Gaudí was convinced that nature was the medium by which the earth became the friend and master of man. Nature inspired the designs of Gaudí.

Expressionist naturalism runs throughout his work. His constructions often appear as living organisms. Gaudí´s sensibility and genius allowed him to live in a world created by his own fantasies.

sens pecat fou concebuda

Gaudí once said, "My soul is not in a hurry." when people asked him with impatience about the works of the Sagrada Família. Gaudí consecrated his architecture and his life to God, and many of his works prove it.

The architect's fervent faith and Catholic devotion greatly influenced his work. His projects became a religious exaltation and an expression of his strong nationalist feelings. The architect's beliefs are evident in buildings like the crypt of Colònia Güell and the Sagrada Família.

# furniture by gaudí

Gaudí's imagination had no limits when it came to designing spaces and buildings. Nevertheless, his work always presented a pronounced rationalism and a deep knowledge of architectural norms. His contributions to the world of furniture design also featured this double virtue: functionality and originality.

Gaudí liked to be fully involved in every aspect of his projects. The pleasure of design inspired him to create furnishings and numerous decorative elements for both interiors and exteriors, including doors, spyholes, knobs, flowerpot holders, railings and balconies.

His furniture designs featured solid forms and simple profiles. In a way, his pieces revived the definitive lines of medieval furnishings, while displaying the lively, sinuous and zigzagging lines that are his trademark.

Gaudí tended to mix styles, which gave his furnishings a personal touch and a sculptural feel. Created in a totally artisan manner, his furniture combined ergonomics with beautiful and well-defined lines, often inspired by organic forms.

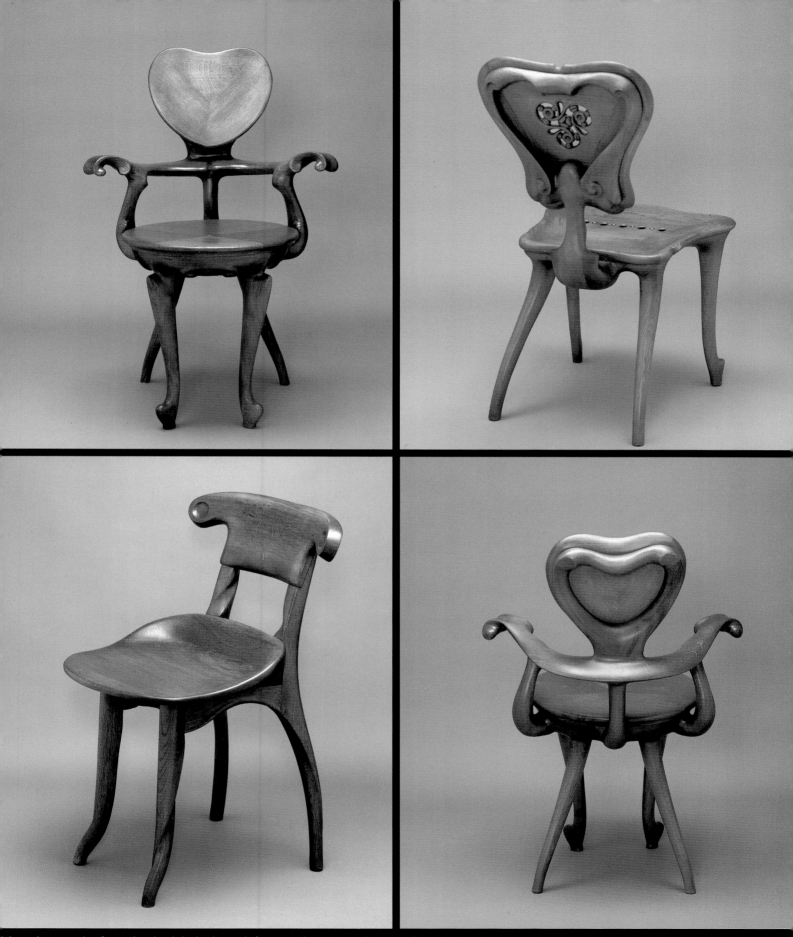

These chairs, made of carved and polished oak wood, feature striking lines and sinuous forms that border on surrealism. The architect designed the chairs for Casa Calvet

The shape of the mirror that Gaudí designed for Casa Calvet -made out of oak wood- achieves a balance between the neo-baroque aesthetic and simple lines.

gaudí by night

No passar
No pasar
No entry

CAIXA CATALUNYA

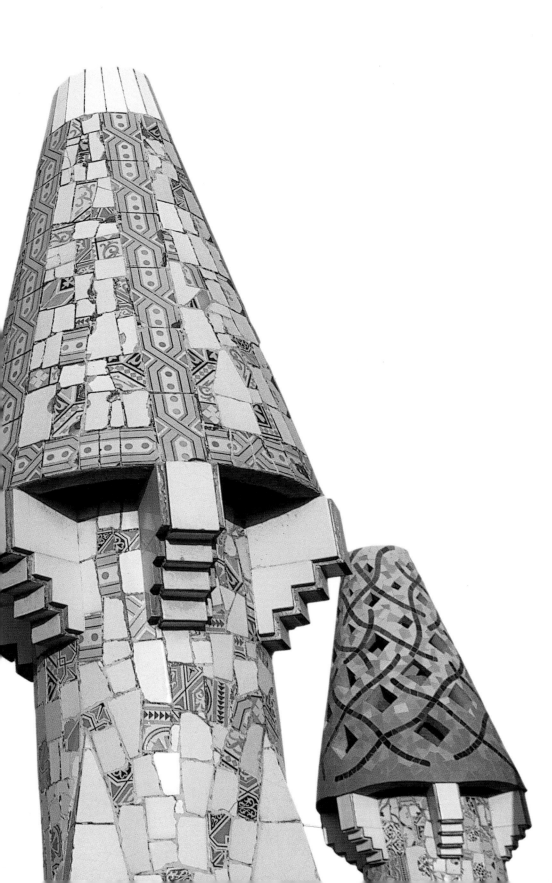

poetic vision

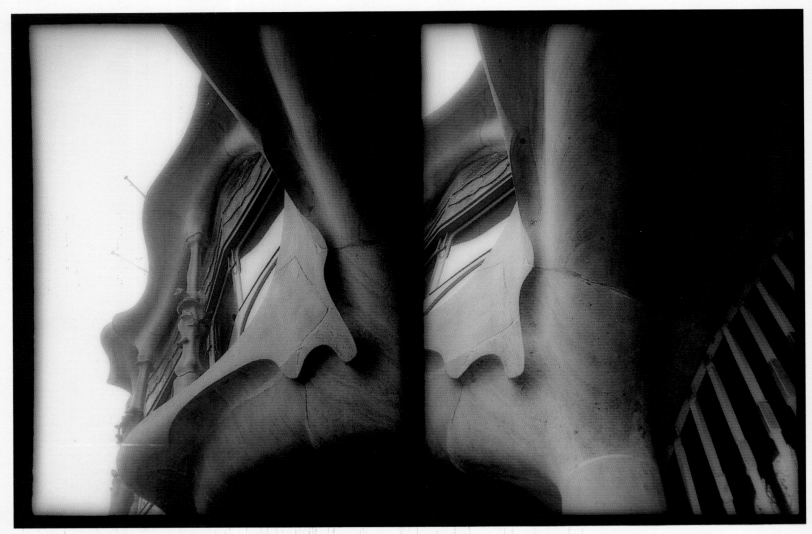

*"Glory is light, light brings happiness, and happiness is the pleasure of the spirit"*

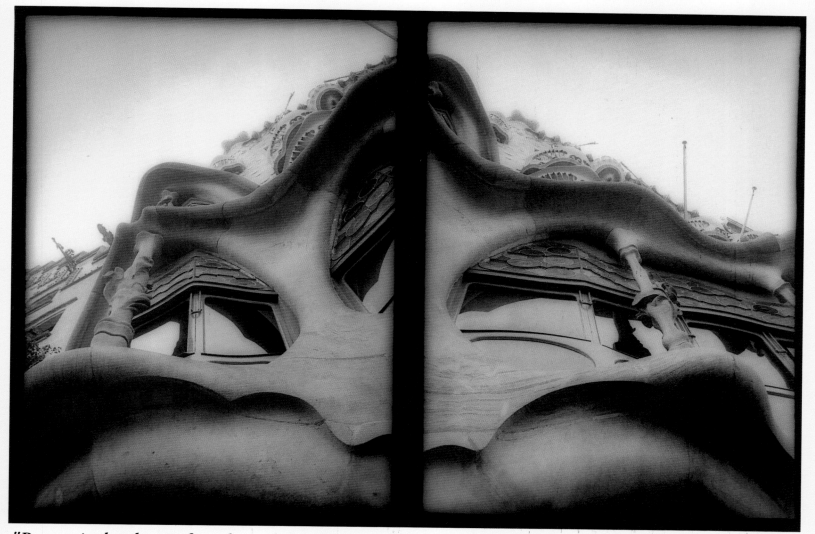

*"Beauty is the gleam of truth, and the gleam captivates everyone; because of this, art has universality"*

*"Originality consists in getting closer to, in returning, to the origin"*

*"Sight is the sense of glory and hearing is the sense of faith"*

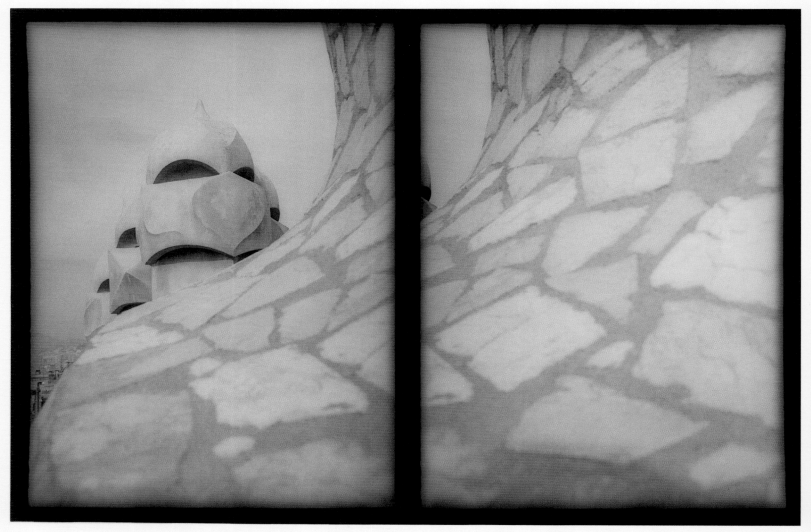

*"Light is the mother of all plastic arts; architecture is the measure and distribution of light"*

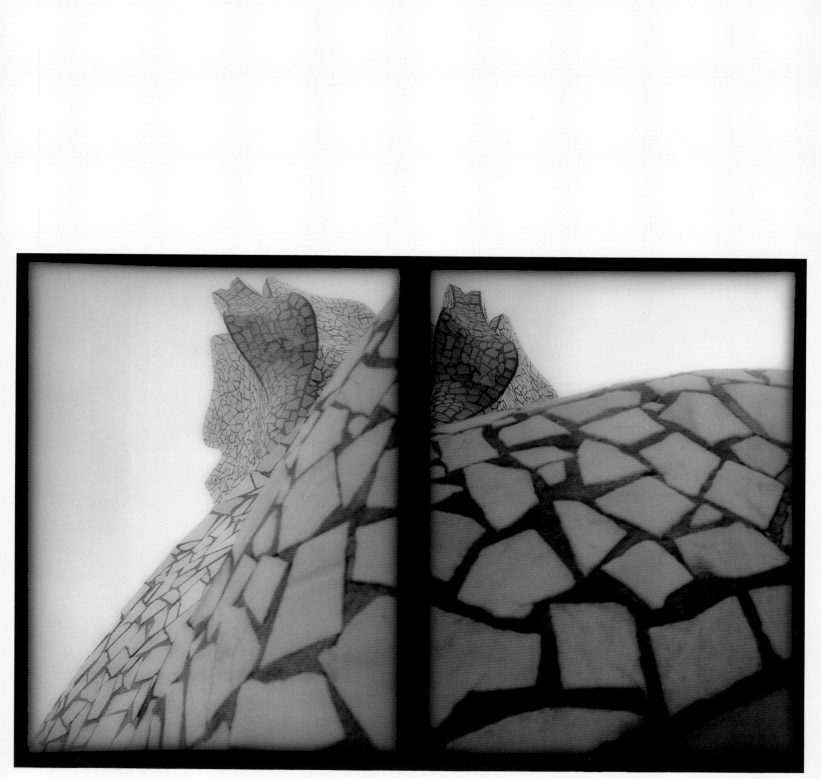

*"All buildings have cracks, like men have sins; what is important is that they are not fatal"*

chronology and bibliography

# chronology of the life and work of antoni gaudí

1852 — Born in Reus, Tarragona; son of Francesc Gaudí i Serra and Antònia Cornet y Bertran.

1867 — First drawings in the magazine "El Arlequín" of Reus, Tarragona.

1867-1870 — Collaborated with Josep Ribera and Eduard Toda on the restoration of the Poblet monastery.

1873-1878 — Studies at the Escuela Técnica Superior d'Arquitectura de Barcelona.

1876 — Design for the Spanish Pavilion of the Exhibition of the Centennial of Philadelphia.
School projects: patio of a Provincial Delegation and a jetty.
Death of his mother.

1877 — Design of a monumental fountain for Plaça Catalunya, Barcelona. Plans for the Hospital General in Barcelona. Designed an auditorium as the final project for his degree.

1878 — Design of the streetlamps for Plaça Reial (inaugurated in September, 1879). Draft of Casa Vicenc. Store window for the glove shop of Esteban Comella, which captured the attention of Eusebi Güell, who became his patron.

1882 — Collaborated with Josep Fontserè on the Parc de la Ciutadella. Gaudí personally designed the entrance doors and the cascade.

1878 -1882 — Design of the Textile Worker's Cooperative of Mataró. Plan for a kiosk for Enrique Girosi.

1879 — Decoration of the pharmacy Gibert on Passeig de Gràcia in Barcelona (demolished in 1895).
The death of his sister Rosita Gaudí de Egea.

1880 — Plan for the electrical illumination of the seawall in collaboration with Josep Serramalera.

1882 — Design of a hunting pavilion commissioned by Eusebi Güell on the coasts of Garraf, Barcelona.

1883 — Drawing of the altar for the Santo Sacramento chapel for the parochial church of Alella, Barcelona.

1883-1888 — House for the tile manufacturer Don Manuel Vicens on the street Carolines in Barcelona. In 1925, the architect Joan Baptista Serra Martínez enlarged the space between two supporting walls, modifying the walls and the property limits.

1883-1885 — House for Don Máximo Díaz de Quijano, widely known as "El Capricho" ("The Caprice"), in Comillas, Santander. The head of construction was Cristóbal Cascante, architect and school companion of Gaudí.

1884-1887 — Pavilions of the Finca Güell: caretaker's quarters and stables on Avenida Pedralbes in Barcelona. The pavilions now house the headquarters of the Real Cátedra Gaudí, inaugurated in 1953, belonging to the Escuela Técnica Superior de Arquitectura de Barcelona.

1883-1926 — Temple expiatori de la Sagrada Familia.

1886-1888 — Palau Güell, residence of Eusebi Güell and his family on the street Nou de La Rambla in Barcelona. Since 1954, the building has housed the headquarters of Barcelona's Museum of Theatre.

1887 — Drawing of the Pavilion of the Transatlantic Company, at the Naval Exhibition in Cádiz.

1888-1889 — Palacio Episcopal de Astorga, León. Gaudí received the assignment from the bishop of Astorga, Joan Baptista Grau i Vallespinós. In 1893, due to the bishop's death, he abandoned the project, which Ricard Guereta later finished.

1889-1893 — Colegio de las Teresianas on the street Ganduxer in Barcelona, commissioned by Enrique d' Ossó, founder of the Order.

| 1892-1893 | The home of Fernández Andrés, widely known as "Casa de los Botines," in León. |
|---|---|
| 1895 | Bodegas Güell on the coasts of Garraf, Barcelona with the collaboration of Francesc Berenguer. |
| 1898-1900 | Casa Calvet, on the street Caspe in Barcelona. |
| 1900-1909 | Home of Jaume Figueres, known as "Bellesguard." Joan Rubió i Bellver helped manage the project. |
| 1900-1914 | Park Güell, on Barcelona's "Bald Mountain," commissioned by Eusebi Güell and with the collaboration of Josep Maria Jujol. In 1922, it became municipal property. |
| 1901-1902 | Door and wall of the estate of Hermenegild Miralles on Passeig Manuel Girona in Barcelona. |
| 1902 | Reform of the house of the Marqués of Castelldosrius, on the street Nova Junta de Comerç in Barcelona. Decoration of Café Torino, commissioned by Ricard Company and with the collaboration of Pere Falqués, Lluís Domènech i Montaner and Josep Puig i Cadafalch. The café, which no longer exists, was located on Passeig de Gràcia in Barcelona. |
| 1903-1914 | Reformation of the Catedral de Palma de Mallorca, commissioned by Pere Campins and with the collaboration of Francesc Berenguer, Joan Rubió i Bellver and Josep Maria Jujol. |
| 1904 | House project for Lluís Graner. |
| 1904-1906 | Reformation of Casa Batlló on Passeig de Gràcia in Barcelona, commissioned by Josep Batlló i Casanovas and with the collaboration of Josep Maria Jujol. |
| 1906 | Death of his father. |
| 1906-1910 | Casa Milà, widely known as "La Pedrera" on Paseo de Gràcia in Barcelona, commissioned by Rosario Segimon de Milà and with the collaboration of Josep Maria Jujol. |
| 1908-1916 | Crypt of the Colònia Güell, in Santa Coloma de Cervelló, Barcelona. Construction began in 1908 and was supervised by Francesc Berenguer. The act of consecration took place November 3, 1915. |
| 1908 | Gaudí received the assignment to construct a hotel in New York, which remained only a sketch. |
| 1909-1910 | Schools of the Temple Expiatori de la Sagrada Família. |
| 1910 | The work of Gaudí is displayed at the Société Nationale de Beaux-Arts in Paris. |
| 1912 | Pulpits for the parochial church of Blanes, Girona. The death of his niece Rosa Egea i Gaudí, 36 years old. |
| 1914 | The death of his friend and collaborator Francesc Berenguer. Decides to work exclusively on the Sagrada Família. |
| 1923 | Studies for the chapel of the Colònia Calvet in Torelló, Barcelona. |
| 1924 | Pulpit for a church in Valencia. |
| 1926 | Gaudí is hit by a tram on June 7 and dies three days later at Hospital de la Santa Creu in Barcelona. |

# bibliography

Bassegoda i Nonell, Joan I., *Gaudí. Arquitectura del futur*. Barcelona, Editorial Salvat para la Caixa de Pensions, 1984.

Castellar-Gassol, Joan, *Gaudí. La vida de un visionario*. Barcelona, Edicions 1984, 1999.

Collins, George R., *Antonio Gaudí*. 1962.

Garcia, Raül, *Barcelona y Gaudí. Ejemplos modernistas*. Barcelona, H. Kliczkowski, 2000.

Garcia, Raül, *Gaudí y el Modernismo en Barcelona*. Barcelona, H. Kliczkowski, 2001.

Güell, Xavier, *Antoni Gaudí*. Barcelona, Ed. Gustavo Gili, 1987.

Lahuerta, J. J., *Gaudí i el seu temps*. Barcelona, Barcanova, 1990.

Llarch, J., *Gaudí, biografía mágica*. Barcelona, Plaza & Janés, 1982.

Martinell, Cèsar, *Gaudí. Su vida, su teoría, su obra*. Barcelona, Col·legi d'Arquitectes de Catalunya, 1967.

Martinell, Cèsar, *"Gaudí i la Sagrada Família comentada per ell mateix"*. Barcelona, Editorial Aymà, 1941.

Morrione, G. *Gaudí. Immagine e architettura*. Roma, Kappa ed., 1979.

Ràfols, J. F. y Folguera, F., *Gaudí*. Barcelona, Editorial Sintes, 1928.

Ràfols, José F., *Gaudí*. Barcelona, Aedos, 1960.

Solà-Morales, Ignasi de, *Gaudí*. Barcelona, Polígrafa cop., 1983.

Torii, Tokutoshi, *El mundo enigmático de Gaudí*. Editorial Castalia, 1983.

Tolosa, Luis, *Barcelona, Gaudí y la Ruta del Modernismo*. Barcelona, H. Kliczkowski, 2000.

Van Zandt, Eleanor, *La vida y obras de Gaudí*. Londres, Parragon Book Service Limited, 1995.

Zerbst, Rainer. *Antoni Gaudí*. Colonia, Benedikt Taschen, 1985.

# web sites of interest

www.barcelona-on-line.es
www.come.to/gaudi
www.cyberspain.com
www.gaudiallgaudi.com
www.gaudiclub.com
www.gaudi2002.bcn.es
www.greatbuildings.com
www.horitzó.es/expo2000
www.reusgaudi2002.org
www.rutamodernisme.com

# acknowledgements

We would like to express our gratitude to Daniel Giralt Miracle, Commissioner of the International Year of Gaudí, for his collaboration with the prologue. To Joan Bassegoda i Nonell, of the Real Cátedra Gaudí, for providing the drawings of most of the projects. To Gabriel Vicenç, for the invaluable information that he provided about the Cathedral of Palma de Mallorca. To the Museu Comarcal Salvador Vilaseca of Reus, for one of the photographs of Antoni Gaudí. To the Arxiu Nacional de Catalunya, for the Brangulí photograph of the architect. To AZ Disseny S.L., which produces and distributes exclusive, exact reproductions of furnishings by Antoni Gaudí. T: T:34932051581 www.cambrabcn.es/gaudi. To the Gaudí Club. And to all the photographers who collaborated on the project.

## location of the buildings in Barcelona

1. casa vicens
2. finca güell
3. sagrada família
4. palau güell
5. colegio de las teresianas

6. casa calvet
7. park güell
8. finca miralles
9. casa batlló
10. casa milà

bellesguard is not on the map

# Other titles by the publishing company

Fundición, 15  Polígono Industrial Santa Ana  28529 Rivas-Vaciamadrid  Madrid  Tel. 34 91 666 50 01  Fax 34 91 301 26 83  asppan@asppan.com  www.onlybook.com

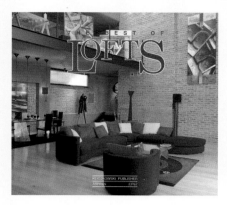

The Best of Lofts
ISBN: (E/GB) 95-09575-84-4

The Best of Bars & Restaurants
ISBN: (E/GB) 95-09575-86-0

The Best of American Houses
ISBN: (E/GB) 98-79778-17-0

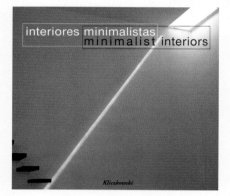

Interiores minimalistas/Minimalist Interiors
ISBN: (E/GB) 98-79778-16-6

Lofts minimalistas/Minimalist lofts
ISBN: (E/GB) 84-89439-55-9

Estancias Argentinas
ISBN: (E) 98-79778-19-7

Guggenheim
ISBN (E): 84-89439-52-4
ISBN (GB): 84-89439-53-2
ISBN (D): 84-89439-54-0
ISBN (P): 84-89439-63-X

Hotels. Designer & Design
Hoteles. Arquitectura y Diseño
ISBN (E/GB): 84-89439-61-3

Cafés. Designer & Design
Cafés. Arquitectura y Diseño
ISBN (E/GB): 84-89439-69-9

E: Spanish text          GB: English text          IT: Italian text          D: German text          P: Portuguese text          J: Japanese text

Pubs
ISBN: (E) 84-89439-68-0

Luis Barragán
ISBN: (E/GB) 987-9474-02-3

Andrea Mantegna
ISBN: (E) 987-9474-10-4

Claude Monet
ISBN: (E) 987-9474-03-1

Rembrandt
ISBN: (E) 987-9474-09-0

Francisco Goya
ISBN: (E) 987-9474-11-2

Álvaro Siza
ISBN: (E) 84-89439-70-2
ISBN: (P) 972-576-220-7

Autos de Cuba
ISBN: (E) 84-89439-62-1

Veleros de época
ISBN (E): 987-9474-06-6

www.onlybook.com

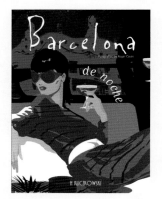

Los encantos de Barcelona/
Barcelona Style
ISBN: (E)    84-89439-56-7
ISBN: (GB) 84-89439-57-5

Barcelona de noche/
Barcelona by night
ISBN: (E)    84-89439-71-0
ISBN: (GB) 84-89439-72-9

Madrid
ISBN: (E)    84-89439-88-5
ISBN: (GB) 84-89439-89-3

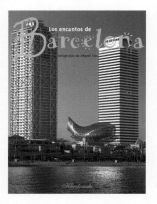

Bauhaus
ISBN: (E) 98-79778-14-2

Antoni Gaudí
ISBN: (E) 98-75130-09-5

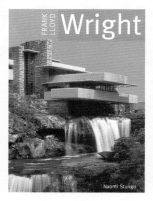

Frank Lloyd Wright
ISBN: (E) 98-79778-11-1

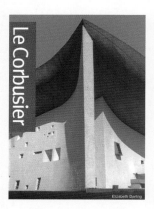

Le Corbusier
ISBN: (E) 98-79778-13-8

Frank Gehry
ISBN: (E) 85868-879-5

La vida y obras de Antoni Gaudí
ISBN: (E) 950-9575-78-X